Grammar and Style Choices for College Writers

This textbook provides a practical guide to grammar and style choices for college writers, giving students a basic vocabulary for thinking and talking about language use and enabling them to make purposeful choices in their writing.

Each section includes a short overview of a grammatical topic accompanied by exercises for raising the students' awareness of and skills in using specific grammatical structures. It focuses on the practical and rhetorical functions of grammatical structures as they are used in expository and analytic writing, rather than on de-contextualized grammatical rules. Students will develop a repertoire of grammatical choices and understand the strategic reasons for making these choices in their writing for various audiences. It particularly attends to the structures that present the most difficulty for college students from multilingual communities and communities where a non-standard dialect of English is used on a daily basis.

This textbook can be used as a core textbook for grammar courses as well as a supplementary text for composition courses. It is also suitable for courses tailored to multilingual, advanced non-native, or non-standard speakers of English.

Olga Griswold is a professor of linguistics and TESOL at California State Polytechnic University at Pomona.

Jennie L. Watson is an instructor of composition at California State Polytechnic University, Pomona and Norco College, California.

Grammar and Style Choices for College Writers

OLGA GRISWOLD AND
JENNIE L. WATSON

Routledge
Taylor & Francis Group

LONDON AND NEW YORK

Cover image: FG Trade / Getty Images

First published 2023
by Routledge
605 Third Avenue, New York, NY 10158

and by Routledge
4 Park Square, Milton Park, Abingdon, Oxon, OX14 4RN

Routledge is an imprint of the Taylor & Francis Group, an informa business

© 2023 Olga Griswold and Jennie L. Watson

Library of Congress Cataloging-in-Publication Data
Names: Griswold, Olga, author. | Watson, Jennie L., author.
Title: Grammar and style choices for college writers / Olga Griswold, Jennie L. Watson.
Description: New York, NY: Routledge, 2023. | Includes bibliographical references and index.
Identifiers: LCCN 2022010365 (print) | LCCN 2022010366 (ebook) | ISBN 9780367748593 (hardback) | ISBN 9780367740689 (paperback) | ISBN 9781003159889 (ebook)
Subjects: LCSH: English language–Grammar. | English language–Rhetoric. | Report writing.
Classification: LCC PE1112 .G685 2023 (print) | LCC PE1112 (ebook) | DDC 428.2–dc23/eng/20220509
LC record available at https://lccn.loc.gov/2022010365
LC ebook record available at https://lccn.loc.gov/2022010366

ISBN: 978-0-367-74859-3 (hbk)
ISBN: 978-0-367-74068-9 (pbk)
ISBN: 978-1-003-15988-9 (ebk)

DOI: 10.4324/9781003159889

Typeset in Charter
by Deanta Global Publishing Services, Chennai, India

Contents

Acknowledgements

In writing and producing this book, we owe our deepest gratitude to many wonderful individuals, without whose help it would not have been possible to complete this project. First and foremost, we are deeply indebted to all the students we have taught over our combined three decades as instructors in higher education. They have both inspired our pedagogical approach and provided models for the instructional materials used here. We are also thankful to our own teachers who, when we were just starting out in our profession, triggered our interest in the teaching of grammar as a rhetorical resource and spurred us to research, explore, create, and implement productive teaching approaches. It is with great appreciation that we would like to acknowledge Marianne Celce-Murcia, Linda Jensen, Donna Brinton, and Christine Holten for their mentorship and encouragement. Our special thanks go to all the authors who have allowed us to use excerpts from their publication for the exercises in this book. Finally, we are deeply grateful to Brian Eschrich, Sean Daly, and the production team at Routledge, who guided us throughout the whole process of publishing a book.

Introduction

How many of us have heard an English teacher say, "We are going to learn some grammar," and issued an exasperated groan? Oh, no! Not grammar! We hate grammar! Grammar is boring! Grammar is hard! And it's totally useless! After all, we've been speaking and writing without any grammar whatsoever almost all of our lives. We don't need to know what the subjunctive mood is or which modals count as epistemic to write an essay or a lab report (and what is a "modal" anyway?). Right? Right? Well, no, we don't need to know the definition of the subjunctive mood, not really. And yes, we kind of do need to know how grammar works in order to write clearly and persuasively. Let us explain.

We can and do communicate in our daily lives without knowing what the subjunctive mood is or what modals are, but we absolutely cannot communicate without grammar. Grammar is a system of patterns (aka "rules") in arranging words into meaningful phrases and sentences. From this system of patterns, we can choose those that help us express our meaning, our attitudes, and our emotions in the best possible way. Everything we say or write is governed by these grammar patterns. If we didn't have them, our speech and writing would resemble a word salad, and we would not be able to understand each other.

Grammar is a remarkably powerful tool. Using a different pattern of arranging words (i.e., a different grammar rule) can completely change the meaning of what we are saying. For example, imagine that you are going to a potluck party, and you are bringing a gallon of your famous potato salad. Once you arrive, the organizer of the party – let's call her Jenna – says, "Only *I* eat potato salad." Your first thought in this case might be, "Uh-oh. I brought too much. Jenna is the only one who will eat some!" But if Jenna says, "I eat *only* potato

DOI: 10.4324/9781003159889-1

salad," you might think, "It's great that I brought a lot! Otherwise, Jenna would have to go hungry. After all, she can't eat anything else, and everybody will be absolutely devouring my delicious potato salad as well!" And if Jenna declares, "I <u>*only*</u> <u>*eat*</u> potato salad," you might wonder, "What a weird thing to say. What else would you do with it but eat it?" You see, by relying on different rules of placing the word "only," we get three sentences that mean three completely different things, even though all these sentences consist of exactly the same words.

"So what?" you might say, "I've been naturally doing this all my life without giving it a second thought. Why do I need to learn the rules for it?" Indeed, when we speak, we don't need to think about grammar much: if the person we are speaking to doesn't understand our message because of a misused grammatical pattern, we can rephrase, clarify, or explain what we mean right then and there. We can also draw on resources other than the spoken words to make ourselves understood – our intonation, body language, facial expressions, and the knowledge of our environment that we share with our conversation partners.

But when we write, none of these non-verbal resources are available to us. We can't correct our word choice on the go, or rearrange the words half-way through a sentence, or point to something while referring to it to make clear what we mean, or change the pitch of our voice to indicate our emotions. We can only rely on words. Yet we still need to make ourselves clear so that our readers can follow our train of thought and understand our ideas. That is why arranging our words – i.e., using grammatical patterns – effectively is key to clear written communication.

When we write for college assignments or for job-related projects, we also need to write in a certain style. This style tends to be more formal than speech. This is when a good understanding of grammar comes in handy. The ability to be both formal and clear at the same time calls for strong skills in choosing the appropriate grammatical patterns deliberately and effectively.

And this is the purpose of this book – to help you gain such skills.

ABOUT THIS BOOK

This book is in many ways different from what might come to your mind when you think "grammar." It's not a dry, pedantic treatise on the evil nature of split infinitives or on the abomination of ending sentences with prepositions. In fact, we do not object to either practice: go ahead, split your infinitives and end your sentences in prepositions if it makes these sentences clear and readable and allows you to emphasize particularly important ideas in your writing.

Neither are we trying to make you memorize a bunch of grammatical jargon. Although we do introduce some grammatical terms in the text, we have tried our best to minimize their use and to call on them only when absolutely necessary to make our explanations concise and unambiguous. Nowhere in the book will you be asked to memorize those terms. Throughout the chapters, we will provide you with examples of grammatical patterns so that you know what they look like, and we will label them so that you know what the labels mean if you see them in other books, on some grammar- and writing-related websites, or in classes where language might be the subject of instruction. But we mainly focus on highlighting the usage and meaning of the key patterns common in the written medium.

Our goal is to help you gain awareness of how different grammatical patterns are used in academic and professional writing, and how you, as a writer, can consciously control and manipulate them to achieve particular rhetorical effects, from focusing your readers' attention on the most important aspects of your text, to expressing your attitude towards the topic you are writing about, to conveying your knowledge, credibility, and professionalism through your writing style.

Throughout the book, we use authentic materials for all practice exercises. By "authentic" we mean materials that appeared in academic, scientific, professional, and popular publications, such as college textbooks, research studies, trade magazine articles, professional blogs, or newspaper opinion pieces and commentaries. We have chosen these materials because they represent real language used by real writers in the real world of academic and professional engagement. As such, they will serve as excellent models for you to emulate and learn from. We have also extensively drawn on the writing of the students we have taught over the past four decades of our combined teaching experience. Many editing and awareness-raising exercises are based on the adaptations of these students' work, for which we are deeply grateful to them.

This book consists of five chapters.

In Chapter 1, you will become familiar with the building blocks of sentences. This chapter will lay a foundation for your ability to compose your own sentences that are fluent, informative, complex, and yet easily readable and understood by your audience. This knowledge will also assist you in revising your drafts and making the first rough sketches of your ideas clearer and the flow from one sentence to another smoother.

Chapter 2 covers the core punctuation rules used in contemporary formal writing. Following these rules will allow you to help your readers separate your ideas into easily understood segments and, as a result, effortlessly grasp the most important aspects of your argument.

Chapter 3 focuses on the verb forms and the patterns of their use in academic writing. Verbs serve as anchors for everything else in the sentence. They are essential in communicating to your readers *when* the action you are writing about is happening, *what kind* of action it is, whether you are *giving an example* of something or *drawing a conclusion*, whether you are referring to an *opinion* or a *fact*, and so on. In addition to facilitating the flow of your text, the appropriate choice of verb forms can effectively indicate to your readers that you are a credible and competent writer.

Chapter 4 addresses the formation of complex noun phrases – a tool strong writers use to compact a lot of information into a small amount of writing and to maintain a professional and objective tone in their work. Complex noun phrases enable writers to "chunk" information for the reader, making the processing of the content easier. Therefore, being able to create and understand them is helpful not only in improving your writing but also in enhancing your ability to read rather dense college-level materials more quickly and with better comprehension.

Chapter 5 focuses on the patterns of texts and sentences that contribute to the clarity of your style as a writer. These patterns include parallelism in the presentation of ideas to show which of them go together, and which ones the reader needs to separate; the effective placement of modifying phrases to clarify who is doing what; and the selection of word forms that best fit the context of your writing. Here you'll also review how to choose between frequently confused words such as "there" vs. "their" or "elude" vs. "allude."

Finally, we hope that after you acquire your advanced grammatical skills by working through this book, you will be able to write eloquent, clear, and sophisticated texts effortlessly. Yet all of us, no matter our level of writing expertise, need to know how to edit our first drafts. For this reason, the book includes appendices with several step-by-step self-editing guides for structures that writers most commonly find confusing or difficult. We encourage you to refer to these guides whenever you need to edit a piece of writing that you plan on submitting to others, be it a class paper, a cover letter for a job, or a report you need to send to your boss or a client at work. Writing well makes the job of reading and understanding your work easier on your audience. And that will always earn you credibility and respect.

HOW TO USE THIS BOOK

Improving your ability to write well and proofread your grammar and punctuation takes more than memorizing a few rules. In order to break some less-than-clear-and-efficient patterns you may have had in your writing for years and to replace them with more effective ones, you need to become aware of what the patterns are and how they convey meaning; you need to understand how and what needs changing; and you need to practice editing. This book uses these methods of raising awareness, gaining understanding, and practicing in order to help you make significant improvements in your writing, correct errors and, more importantly, make you more comfortable writing in advanced academic or professional settings. These skills must be learned by *doing,* by actively practicing them, and not by simply skimming though the chapters. For this reason, this book is designed like a workbook. You will be asked not only to read information, but to actively engage with the materials so that you can identify what strong writers do, understand how your choices affect your meaning and your credibility, and implement your knowledge into your own writing.

Complete the practices. Some practices you may find easy, and others will cause you to think and sometimes struggle. Both of these processes can be helpful to your learning. We have worked to design the practices so that you can either write directly in the book or respond on a separate paper or document (often with numbered responses).

Read the summaries. The summaries are usually in a table form or a chart so that you can use them to understand the information initially or so that you can return and review it quickly to refresh your knowledge.

Talk about the information. We have discussions built into some of the practices because verbally explaining your (or another writer's) choices can help you to better understand and remember the information.

In short, don't just read this book. Use and work through this book with a writing utensil in your hand so that you can actively learn, practice, and improve your skills.

Now, onward to the grammar adventure!

1 Understanding Sentence Parts

Every time you write a sentence, you include two parts in it:

1. You state who or what the sentence is about. This is called a *subject*.
2. And you tell your reader something about this subject. This is called a *verb phrase* (or *predicate*).

Without both of these parts, the sentence will be incomplete because it cannot convey the entire idea the writer is setting out to convey.

For example, when you write:

The laws of physics are surprisingly few in number[1]

you indicate to the reader that your sentence is about ***the laws of physics***, and what the reader needs to know is that there are not many of them – they ***are surprisingly few in number***.

In this sentence, ***the laws of physics*** is the subject, and ***are surprisingly few in number*** is the verb phrase.

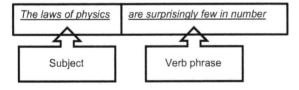

This example sentence is rather short and contains important and complete but fairly brief information.

Most of the time, however, the documents we write in the real world – whether a lab report at school or an email to a client at work – need to be more informative. Therefore, the sentences in them need to include more details: where, when, how, or why the events take place or to whom they are happening. These bits of information

DOI: 10.4324/9781003159889-2

are included in the verb phrase and are expressed by a variety of word groups. Some of these word groups are *objects*, and some are *adverbials*.

In this chapter, we will explore:

- How to make sure that your sentences always express complete ideas, i.e., that they have proper subjects and verb phrases
- And how to add important details to your sentences using objects and adverbials so that your readers can understand your main points and the necessary information you want them to gain from your texts.

This chapter consists of three sections. Each section addresses a particular skill in building complete and informative sentences:

1.1   Building sentences with clear subjects
1.2   Ensuring that the verb form matches its subject
1.3   Adding clear and necessary details to the basic sentence frame

Let's begin.

1.1 WHAT KINDS OF SUBJECTS
   CAN SENTENCES HAVE?

After you work through this section of the chapter, you will be well on the way to say confidently:

◎ I know what kind of phrases can be used as subjects of sentences.

◎ I can edit my own writing to ensure that all sentences have proper subjects and verb phrases and express complete ideas.

 ## STRATEGIES: IDENTIFYING
   SUBJECTS OF SENTENCES

Strategy	Examples	Explanation
Turn the sentence into a question.	For example, _a pilot_ **should** _understand the effect of wind forces on the flight path._[2] For example, what **should** _a pilot_ understand?	When we turn the sentence into a question, the subject will swap places with the first word in the verb phrase. In the sentence here, the word _should_ – the first word in the verb phrase – goes in front of the phrase _a pilot_, but not in front of the phrase _for example_.
Ask: Who or what is doing the action in the sentence?	_The laws of physics are few in number._ What is/are few in number? – _The laws of physics_.	The answer to this question is the subject. In the example, the phrase _The laws of physics_ answers the question _What is few in number?_ Therefore, it is the subject of the sentence.
Add a "tag" question to the sentence	For example, **a pilot** should understand the effects of wind forces on the flight path, shouldn't **he (or she)**? **The laws of physics** are surprisingly few in number, aren't **they**?	When we add such a tag question, the pronoun in it – the word like **he, she, it,** or **they** – will replace the subject. In the example sentences, the word _he_ (or _she_) will replace the phrase _a pilot_, and the word _they_ will replace the phrase _the laws of physics_. We can, therefore, conclude that _a pilot_ and _the laws of physics_ are the subjects of their respective sentences.

PRACTICE 1.1-A

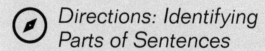

Directions: Identifying Parts of Sentences

The purpose of this exercise is to draw your attention to the subjects of sentences in the types of texts you read and write in your classes. Sometimes, the subjects will be the first word or words in a sentence, and sometimes not.

- Study the Strategy Table above and learn three ways of finding a complete subject in a sentence.
- Use the strategies to find subjects in every sentence in the text below. You can use one strategy at a time or try and apply more than one to make sure you found the right subject.
- Then, fill in the table below the text for each sentence. Sentences 1 and 2 are done for you as an example.

Text:

From: Urone, P. P., & Hinrichs, R. (2020). *College physics.* Rice University Open Stacks. Available for free at https://openstax.org/details/books/college-physics.

(1) The physical universe is enormously complex in its detail. (2) Every day, each of us observes a great variety of objects and phenomena. (3) Over the centuries, the curiosity of the human race has led us collectively to explore and catalog a tremendous wealth of information. (4) From the flight of birds to the colors of flowers, from lightning to gravity, from quarks to clusters of galaxies, from the flow of time to the mystery of the creation of the universe, we have asked questions and assembled huge arrays of facts. (5) In the face of all these details, we have discovered that a surprisingly small and unified set of physical laws can explain what we observe. (6) As humans, we make generalizations and seek order. (7) We have found that nature is remarkably cooperative – (8) it exhibits the underlying order and simplicity we so value.

	Introductory Phrase	Subject	Verb Phrase (Predicate)
1	–	The physical universe	is enormously complex in its detail.
2	Every day,	each of us	observes a great variety of objects and phenomena.
3			
4			
5			
6			
7			
8			

PRACTICE 1.1-B

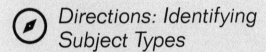

Directions: Identifying Subject Types

This exercise will help you figure out what kind of phrases can act as subjects. The sentences below have been excerpted from different texts, ranging from textbooks and scientific articles to popular media and newspapers.[3]

Find the subject of each underlined verb. When you have found all subjects, study their forms and then place them into one of the three categories in the table below:

- A phrase where the main word is a noun (underline the main noun)
- A single pronoun (*I, you, we, he, she, it, they*) that refers to some other word, word group, or an entity in the world
- An -ing phrase
- The place-holder pronoun *it* in sentences about emotions, time, weather, or distance.

Optional: Work with a partner or small group.

The first three sentences have been done for you as examples. A different strategy of finding the subject has been used in each of the three. You may apply whatever strategy that you find the easiest to use.

Note: You may find that some sentences seem to have more than one subject. That is okay. Some of these sentences contain more than one clause – a concept we will discuss in Chapter 2. If you find more than one subject per sentence, it is definitely worth discussing this with your group and your teacher to see how multiple subjects work.

1. A model is a representation of something that is often too difficult (or impossible) to display directly.
   Make a question: Is a model a representation of something that is difficult to display directly?
   Find the word of phrase that swaps places with the first verb: Is a model...
   Subject – a model

2. Understanding this law makes it easier to learn about the various forms of energy.
   Add a tag: Understanding this law makes it easier to learn about various forms of energy, doesn't it?
   What does "it" replace? – Understanding this law
   Subject – understanding this law

3. Renewable Energy Sources (RES) are playing an increasing role in modern electric power systems.
   Ask who/what: What is playing an increasing role in modern electric power systems? – Renewable Energy Sources (RES).
   *Which phrase answers the **what/who** question? – Renewable Energy Sources (RES)*
   Subject – Renewable Energy Sources (RES)

4. The renewable energy source closest to becoming competitive on the market is wind power.

5. It is five minutes to midnight on New Year's Eve.

6. Some of the most spectacular advances in science have been made in modern physics.

7. The program performs energy balance calculations for each configuration.

8. It then determines the feasibility of each configuration.

9. After simulating all possible system configurations, the program displays a list of configurations sorted by the total cost.

10. It appears that none of the prototype designs will be put to use any time soon.

11. Estimating the wind speed at a certain height is outside of the scope for this paper.

12. Parent-child book reading in infancy increases children's vocabulary by the time of school entry.

13. It is encouraging to know that educational leaders take the problem of bias in the classrooms seriously.

14. By making caregiving a women's problem, companies avoid changing their cultures in ways that would give everyone more life-work balance.

15. Making the resources and testing available at the local level has become a priority for the public officials.

	Subject	Subject Type
1	A **model**	A phrase with a noun as the main word
2	**Understanding** this law	-ing phrase
3	Renewable Energy **Sources** (RES)	A phrase with a noun as the main word
4		
5		
6		
7		
8		
9		
10		
11		
12		
13		
14		
15		

 ## SUMMARY: SUBJECTS OF SENTENCES

- Every sentence must have two parts:
  - Subject – who or what the sentence is about and
  - Verb phrase (predicate) – information about the subject.
- Subjects are not always the first words in a sentence. An introductory phrase may come before the subject. This phrase usually serves to link the ideas in its own sentence with the ideas in the previous sentence.
  - Subjects cannot start with prepositions – words like *by, after, until, with*, and so on. If the first phrase in a sentence begins with such a word, it is an introductory phrase and not the subject.
- Subjects may be expressed by a single personal pronoun, a phrase that has a noun as its main word, an -ing phrase, or the place-holder pronoun *it* in sentences describing time, weather, or the ambient environment.

Using different types of subjects in your sentences helps you **create variety** in your paragraphs so that you don't sound repetitive, and it helps you **connect ideas** throughout your paragraph or essay as you use pronouns and -ing phrases that refer to people, items, or actions you've previously mentioned.

Subject Form	Example
A personal pronoun that refers to another word, word group, or entity in the world: *I, you, we, he, she, it, they*	The program performs energy balance calculations for each configuration. *It* then determines the feasibility of each configuration. Models are very useful in modern science. *They* allow us to conceptualize complex phenomena. *We* can conceptualize the phenomena we cannot experience by using models.
A phrase in which a **noun** is the main word	*The **laws** of physics are surprisingly few in number.* *The renewable energy **source** closest to becoming competitive on the market is wind power.* *Eye **contact** between a parent and a child* promotes mutual regulation of interest.
An -ing phrase	***Understanding** this law* makes it easier to learn about various forms of energy. ***Making** homes available* for working-class Americans is our priority. ***Running** a company successfully* means being able to plan and follow through on every decision.
The place-holder pronoun *it*	*It* is five minutes to midnight on New Year's Eve. *It* has been frustrating to see all these great ideas and not have the resources to implement them.

 # EDITING TECHNIQUES FOR SUBJECTS

Problem	Example	How to Correct the Problem
The subject -ing phrase starts with a preposition (like *by, with, after, until, in*).	**By reducing taxes can increase the amount of government debt.*	**Option 1:** Remove the preposition from the -ing phrase. The -ing phrase becomes the subject: *Reducing taxes can increase the amount of government debt.* **Option 2:** Make the preposition + -ing phrase an introductory phrase and insert a different subject that works in the context: *By reducing taxes, the government can increase the amount of its debt.* Note: This option may require additional changes, such as changing the verb form, or replacing a full noun with a pronoun.

(Continued)

Problem	Example	How to Correct the Problem
A fragment with an implied but not stated subject.	*At the time, experimental quantum computing was brand new. *Just started to take off.*	**Option 1:** Add a pronoun or a phrase with a noun as the main word to the sentence: *At the time, experimental quantum computing was brand new. <u>It</u> just started to take off.* **Option 2:** Turn the subject-less fragment into an -ing phrase and attach it to the complete sentence: *At the time, experimental quantum computing was brand new, <u>just starting</u> to take off.*
A verb after *because, after, until, when,* etc. has an implied but not stated subject.	**Energy from cooked foods was crucial for human evolution because <u>fueled</u> brain expansion in our ancestor species.*	**Option 1:** Add a pronoun or a phrase with a noun as the main word before the verb and after *because (after, until, when,* etc.): *Energy from cooked foods was crucial for human evolution because <u>it</u> fueled brain expansion in our ancestor species.* *Energy from cooked foods was crucial for human evolution because <u>the consumption of such food</u> fueled brain expansion in our ancestor species.* **Option 2:** Remove the connecting word and turn the remaining verb phrase into an -ing phrase: *Energy from cooked foods was crucial for human evolution, <u>fueling</u> brain expansion in our ancestor species.*
A plain verb is used instead of an -ing phrase as the subject.	**<u>Maintain</u> a peaceful and harmonious environment in the workplace is part of a manager's job.*	**Option 1:** Turn the plain verb into an -ing phrase: *<u>Maintaining</u> a peaceful and harmonious environment in the workplace is part of a manager's job.* **Option 2:** Rearrange the sentence and add the word *to* before the plain verb in question: *Part of a manager's job is <u>to maintain</u> a peaceful and harmonious environment in the workplace.*

PRACTICE 1.1-C

 Directions: Editing

The goal of this exercise is to help you practice editing skills. The text below has been adapted from a student essay on the importance of their major (Chemistry). Most of the sentences in the passage are correct, but some are missing subjects or use subjects in the incorrect form.

- Identify subjects in all sentences in the text. Highlight or underline these subjects. (The first one is done for you).
- If the subject is missing or has an inappropriate form, **correct the problem** using one of the techniques outlined in the Editing Techniques above. (Do not make changes for style or punctuation).

Chemistry has always been upheld as one of the essential sciences. By choosing to major in chemistry exposes students to topics that offer a glimpse of the varying career choices available to potential chemists. If you major in chemistry, the prospective employers in the chemical industry will see that you gained practical skills and mastery of the subject. The undergraduate study of chemistry offers students the basic knowledge in hands-on quantitative and qualitative skills. These skills are requisites to almost all graduate level degrees. Subjects like biochemistry and organic chemistry are also required for professional schools, such as medicine. Many chemistry courses are very in-depth and diverse because they are mandatory for other majors in the animal health sciences and biological science.

Chemistry majors also must take many quantitative courses. This set of classes involves the use of instruments to analyze chemicals in trace amounts. These techniques are often used for many industrial purposes, such as quality control. Toy manufacturers rely on analytical chemists to test the lead levels in toys. Food manufacturing companies hire the same chemists to test for toxins before put their products on the market. The analytical techniques that are shown in crime-fighting shows, such as *CSI*, where lab technicians gather evidence and put the evidence through GC-MS for sampling, are taught in the chemistry major. Such skills are also needed by many government agencies because require the understanding of both the concepts of dilution and the principles behind these instruments.

For example, the Metropolitan Water District, the Department of Agriculture, and the Department of Homeland Security routinely hire chemistry students as interns based on their grades during the one year of analytical classes. By developing competent knowledge of instrument operation can then be trained by government agencies to further test for toxins and narcotics.

PRACTICE 1.1-D

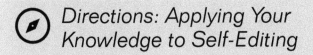 Directions: Applying Your Knowledge to Self-Editing

It's time to apply your understanding of how subjects work in sentences to your own writing. Choose a text that you wrote before for this or any other class. The text must be at least 300 words long. If you do not have a text of 300 words or more, you may choose to work with several shorter texts. Apply the techniques for finding subjects in all the sentences in your text. If you find a sentence with a missing or problematic subject, correct the sentence using one of the editing techniques presented in this section of the chapter.

1.2 HOW DO I MAKE THE VERBS MATCH THE SUBJECTS OF MY SENTENCES?

After you work through this section of the chapter, you will be well on the way to say confidently:

- I know how to match verbs to the subjects of sentences.

- I can edit my own writing to ensure that the verbs in all my sentences match the subjects.

PRACTICE 1.2-A

From: National Heart, Lung, and Blood Institute. (2020, December 3). Asthma. www.nhlbi.nih.gov/health-topics/asthma.

⊘ *Directions: Identifying Usage Patterns*

The purpose of this exercise is to draw your attention to how verbs change to match the subject of the sentence.

- Read the passage below.
- The subjects and verbs in each sentence have been highlighted in bold. Identify which subject goes with which verb.
- Fill in the table below the text to identify the subjects that are used with the verbs listed.

Asthma is a chronic (long-term) condition that **affects** the airways in the lungs. The **airways are** tubes that carry air in and out of your lungs. If **you have** asthma, the **airways can become** inflamed and narrowed at times.

[...]

The exact **cause** of asthma **is** unknown, and the **causes may vary** from person to person. However, **asthma is** often the result of a strong response of the immune system to a substance in the lungs.

[...]

Normally, **the body's immune system helps** to fight infections. Sometimes **a person's immune system responds** to a substance in the environment called an allergen. When **someone breathes** in an allergen, such as ragweed, the immune **system** in the airways **may react** strongly. Other people exposed to the same substance may not react at all.

The immune **system reacts** to an allergen by creating inflammation. **Inflammation makes** your airways swell and narrow and possibly produce more mucus. This can make it harder to breathe.

Subjects with the Verb + s or -es	Subjects with the Verb Is or Has	Subjects with the Verbs Are or Have	Subjects with the Verbs Can + Verb or May + Verb

SUMMARY: MATCHING VERBS WITH SUBJECTS

Chapter 3 will show verb forms in detail. The table below shows which subjects should be used with the base verb (or *be* and *have*) and which should be used with the base verb + -s or -es (or other irregular forms, like *is, are,* or *has*).

By "base verb," we mean the form of verbs when they are listed in the dictionary or the form they take after the word *to*. For example, if we use some of the verbs from the reading above, we find the base verbs *affect, have, become, vary, help, react, respond,* and *breathe*.

There are some irregular verbs with unpredictable patterns. For example, we say, "I *am* happy," "she *is* happy," and "they *are* happy," and "*to be* happy," so although the verb changes to all these different forms, the base form of this verb is *be*.

Type of Subject	Verb Form	Example
Subjects that refer to *one* person, place, thing, or idea Pronouns *he, she,* or *it*	base verb +-s or -es* *Also, irregular verbs, like *is* or *has*	Around the world, the **free market rewards** competition while **concern for the public good is** relegated to the family, houses of worship, or activism.
Subjects that refer to *more than one* person, place, thing, or idea Pronouns *you, we, they*	base verb** **Also, irregular verbs, like *are*	Some **critics argue** that false disease categories are being invented for the aim of profit.
Nouns that refer to **a group** of people, places, things, or ideas • These nouns (like *dozen, decade, team, audience, family*) tend to be treated like subjects that refer to **one** item. **Exceptions:** Some nouns that refer to groups, like *police* or *faculty*, are used with a **base verb**.	base verb +-s or -es*	The **21st century appears** to be unfriendly to businesses. **A just and ethical society offers** equal access to power to all of its citizens. Exception: **Our faculty participate** in teaching, research, and industry outreach to advance our mission.

(Continued)

Type of Subject	Verb Form	Example
Nouns that **cannot be counted**, or that do not have a different form for singular or plural • These nouns (like *research*, *equipment*, and *homework*) can refer to many items, but they don't change form when you have one or more. For example, most humans have two lun**gs**, but if they have *inflammation* in multiple airways, they don't have two inflammation**s** – they just have inflammation.	base verb +-s or -es*	**This advice** <u>applies</u> throughout the industry, but health insurers are more sensitive to litigation. As an electrolyte, **potassium** <u>regulates</u> bodily fluids and enhances muscle control. **Chicago public transportation** <u>provides</u> a high degree of accessibility to people with disabilities.
Subjects that join **two or more nouns** that refer to one person, place, thing, or idea with *and* • Together these nouns can be replaced with the pronoun *they*.	base verb**	When **coral and algae** no longer <u>support</u> each other, the coral turns a ghostly white color. **Baseball, football, and basketball** <u>make</u> up the three most popular sports in the United States today.
Subjects that begin with **every** or **each** and then join two or more nouns that refer to one person, place, thing, or idea with **and** • The words *every* or *each* emphasize the nouns individually.	base verb +-s or -es*	**Each patient and family** <u>is</u> unique, and "family" is defined by the patient, not healthcare providers. For first-time parents, **every day and night** <u>brings</u> new challenges.
Subjects with the patterns below: • Either _____ or _____ • Neither _____ nor _____ • Not only _____ but also _____	Match the verb to the subject that is closer to the verb	**Neither drugs nor alcohol** <u>is</u> suspected in the investigation.
Subjects with the patterns below: • _____ + including • _____ + in addition to • _____ + especially • _____ + as well as • _____ + along with • _____ + together with	Match the verb to the main subject (not to the added information)	**Comments including** profanity or objectionable language <u>are</u> not allowed. **Preschool children** as well as adults <u>exhibit</u> a theory of mind.

(Continued)

Type of Subject	Verb Form	Example
Subjects consisting of any of these words: • Each, either, neither, • Anyone, anybody, anything, • Everyone, everybody, everything, • No one, nobody, nothing, • Someone, somebody, something	base verb +-s or -es*	Although these two constellations contrast greatly, **each offers** a wide array of astronomical objects to study. Somehow **everyone knows** this unwritten rule.
Subjects with the patterns below: • *Here* [verb] _____ • *There* [verb] _____ Note: The words *here* and *there* are never the subject of the sentence. The typical word order is switched, so the subject comes after the verb.	Match the verb to the noun after the verb	Here **is the interesting thing**: the entire world's population could fit shoulder-to-shoulder inside Los Angeles. There **are 27,000 locations** in roughly 70 countries around the world.
Subjects with an **-ing phrase** Subjects with two or more -ing phrases joined with *and*	base verb +-s or -es* base verb**	**Exercising** regularly **lowers** the risk of developing type 2 diabetes. **Maintaining an ideal weight and exercising** regularly **lower** the risk of developing type 2 diabetes.
All kinds of subjects followed by the following special verbs • Can, could, • Should, • Will, would, • May, must, might	base verb	**Public benefits can result** when people pursue what comes easiest: self-interest. **The 40,000 square feet of additional space will allow** the Museum of Modern Art to focus new attention on works by women, Latinos, Asians, and African Americans.

PRACTICE 1.2-B

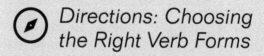

Directions: Choosing the Right Verb Forms

In this practice, you will identify the verb form that matches the type of subject in the sentence. For each sentence, choose one of the two verb forms that best fits the subject. Use the table above to help you.

1. Apart from Antarctica, rice <u>grows/grow</u> on every continent in more than 100 countries.
2. The executive committee <u>meets/meet</u> each month to consider the needs of patients and the hospital and donates money to provide items requested.
3. There <u>is/are</u> currently more than 325,000 undergraduate women involved in Greek life across the country.
4. Every student and teacher <u>uses/use</u> technology every day as a critical tool to personalize and accelerate learning.
5. Customers and banks agree; neither <u>wants/want</u> to resolve financial issues or divulge personal information online.
6. The gas to and from the bank, as well as time spent waiting to process the transaction, <u>adds/add</u> up to thousands of dollars lost.
7. Services including housing, job training, and victim compensation <u>is/are</u> available to trafficking victims.
8. Senate Democrats believe that everyone <u>deserves/deserve</u> a good paying job and a dignified retirement in later life.
9. Not only funds but also valuable human intelligence <u>is/are</u> wasted on intricate weapons that nobody wants to use.
10. Neither men nor women <u>wants/want</u> to pay to keep their belongings at a run-down facility.

PRACTICE 1.2-C

 Directions: Editing

The purpose of this exercise is to help you practice editing for verb forms that don't match the subject of the sentence. The text below has been adapted from a student essay on the ethics of showing instances of substance abuse on social media. Many of the sentences in the passage are correct, but some verb forms do not match the subject.

- Read the text carefully first without focusing on grammar.
- Then, go back to the beginning and read each sentence, identifying the subject and the verb.
- Make sure that the verb matches the subject.
- If the verb and subject do not match, correct either the verb or the subject – whichever makes the sentence clearer and better fitting the context of the essay.

There's societal expectations about how people should act around children, but a chasm has formed since the advent of the internet. When adults take part in social events, they fail to recognize the effects that sharing those events online could have on younger or underage users of social media. A research group from the University of Utah have found that sharing alcohol and substance use on Twitter correlates with areas of lower social and economic standing. The online presence of substance use has the potential to normalize and even glorify risky behaviors. Posting the use of substances and allowing these actions to be seen by younger, unintended audiences on social media is both unethical.

Most social media are more popular among younger age groups, which means that ideas and actions present on social media have a greater probability of being seen by and negatively affecting minors. Although many platforms require that users acknowledge meeting an age requirement, the use of hashtags or keywords such as "prom," "exam," or "school" combined with words such as "alcohol" or "weed" indicate Twitter accounts that belong to underage substance users. Twitter do not actively seek and delete accounts that belong to underage users, but there is an option that allows current users to report users who they believe to be underage (Weng). With teenagers, young adults, and adults using the same social media platforms for communication and entertainment, there becomes more and more undiscovered underage users who is influenced by posts of open use of substances.

The widespread use of social media in the lives of later generations results in ideas having a greater and broader reach. An experimental study determined trends regarding substance use. Because alcohol was the number one most tweeted substance with marijuana following closely behind, these two materials were followed most closely and had the most significant effect on viewers. The central question became whether or not these posts have an impact on under-age users by normalizing and glorifying the use of substances and volatile habits. A recent study that collected nearly 12 million alcohol-related tweets has found that the number of pro-drinking tweets exceeded the number of anti-drinking tweets by 10 times (Weng). While most of these tweets may have no bad intentions, they still implant the idea that such actions are acceptable to underage onlookers.

PRACTICE 1.2-D

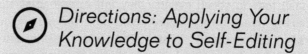 *Directions: Applying Your Knowledge to Self-Editing*

It's time to apply your understanding of how subjects work in sentences to your own writing. Choose a text that you wrote before for this or any other class. The text must be at least 300 words long. If you do not have a text of 300 words or more, you may choose to work with several shorter texts.

1.3 HOW DO I ADD DETAILS TO SENTENCES?

After you work through this section of the chapter, you will be well on the way to say confidently:

◎ I know how to add details to my sentences (with adverbials).

◎ I can edit my own writing to add details and specificity to my sentences.

PRACTICE 1.3-A

From: National Park Service. (2020, September 18). Fort Point: History & culture. www.nps.gov/fopo/learn/historyculture/index .htm

⊘ Directions: Identifying Usage Patterns

The purpose of this exercise is to draw your attention to the details writers can add to sentences and the kind of information they provide.

- Read the two excerpts below about Fort Point, which is a stone building on the southern side of the Golden Gate at the entrance to San Francisco Bay in California.
- Reading 2 is the original passage. Reading 1 has the same information but has been modified to remove some of the details.
- Underline the phrases indicating additional information in Reading 2.
- Then fill out the table below to determine what kind of information the phrases add.
- The first sentence has been done for you. Use your answers to help you discuss the questions at the end with a partner or small group.

Reading 1	Reading 2
Fort Point has stood guard at the narrows of the Golden Gate Bridge. The Fort has been called "the pride of the Pacific," "the Gibraltar of the West Coast," and "one of the most perfect models of masonry in America." When construction began, Fort Point was planned as the most formidable deterrence America could offer. Although its guns never fired a shot, the "Fort at Fort Point" as it was named has witnessed Civil War, obsolescence, earthquake, bridge construction, reuse, and preservation.	Fort Point has stood guard at the narrows of the Golden Gate Bridge in San Francisco, California for over 150 years. The Fort has been called "the pride of the Pacific," "the Gibraltar of the West Coast," and "one of the most perfect models of masonry in America." When construction began during the height of the California Gold Rush, Fort Point was planned as the most formidable deterrence America could offer to a naval attack on California. Although its guns never fired a shot in anger, the "Fort at Fort Point" as it was originally named has witnessed Civil War, obsolescence, earthquake, bridge construction, reuse for World War II, and preservation as a National Historic Site.
Fort Point was built as part of a defense system of forts. Designed at the height of the Gold Rush, the Fort and its companion fortifications would protect the Bay's important commercial and military installations. The Fort was built in the Army's traditional "Third System" style of military architecture (a standard adopted) and would be the only fortification of this impressive design. This fact bears testimony to the importance the military gave San Francisco and the gold fields.	Fort Point was built between 1853 and 1861 by the U.S. Army Engineers as part of a defense system of forts planned for the protection of San Francisco Bay for the Civil War. Designed at the height of the Gold Rush, the Fort and its companion fortifications would protect the Bay's important commercial and military installations against foreign attack. The Fort was built in the Army's traditional "Third System" style of military architecture (a standard adopted in the 1820s) and would be the only fortification of this impressive design constructed west of the Mississippi River. This fact bears testimony to the importance the military gave San Francisco and the gold fields during the 1850s.
Fort Point became underutilized and was used intermittently. The pre-Civil War cannons, so valuable when they were installed, became obsolete and were removed.	In the years after the Civil War, Fort Point became underutilized and was used intermittently as an army barracks. The pre-Civil War cannons, so valuable when they were initially installed, became obsolete and were eventually removed.
Although Fort Point never saw battle, the building has tremendous significance.	Although Fort Point never saw battle, the building has tremendous significance due to its military history, architecture, and association with maritime history.

Meaning	Phrases
When	*for over 150 years*
Where	*in San Francisco, California*
How	
Why	
How often	

Discussion Questions	Answer
How does the added information in Reading 2 affect the sentences, paragraphs, and the overall text?	
Why should writers add details of *when, where, how, why*, and *how often* in their writing?	

⚡ SUMMARY: ADDING DETAILS (ADVERBIALS)

These added details of when, where, how, why, and how often (*adverbials*) can be a single word or a phrase. They can be added as an introductory phrase or included with the verb phrase (in the predicate).

Meaning	Common Details
When	• *for* or ***during*** a length of time • *at* or ***since*** a specific time • *in* a time period • *before* or ***after*** a time or period • ***between*** two points in time • specific time marker (e.g., today) • *-ly* word

Meaning	Common Details
Where	• *at* a location • *in* a location or setting • *on, under, over, through* a location • specific location marker (e.g., here)
How	• *-ly* word • *in* a certain way • *as a certain function* • *by* certain means
Why	• *for* a person or purpose • *to* achieve a purpose • *because or since* reason (sentence) • *because of* something or someone • *due to* a reason or person • *so that* purpose(sentence)
How often	• *-ly* word • *every* or *each* (repeated) time

PRACTICE 1.3-B

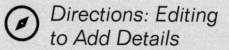

Directions: Editing to Add Details

In this exercise, you will practice adding details (adverbials) to a text to specify and clarify meanings, connect ideas, and engage readers. The text below is adapted from a student essay describing online videos called mukbangs, which show people eating.

• Read the entire text first, noting places where some additional information may make the text more interesting, persuasive, or complete.

• Then add details to the text to show *when, where, how, why,* and *how often* (adverbials). It is up to you what kind of details you want to add.

• You may not need to add details to every sentence, and you may add more than one to some sentences. The choice of details will vary from student to student. There is no one correct answer to this exercise.

• Remember that you can include some as introductory phrases and some phrases as part of the verb phrase (predicate).

Social media and the Internet affect our lives. All the new trends that become relevant come from the Internet. There has been a spike in the use of social media and how much of our lives we put into scrolling or watching videos. One type of video that has become popular is a video style called Mukbangs. A mukbang video is a recording of a content creator who sits down and eats food.

Mukbangs are a trend on YouTube which became popular. When creating these kinds of videos, they display an array of foods. Although in some mukbangs the YouTubers do not talk, in others they do talk. They explain what the food is and what they like about it. The eaters promote the food they are eating and expose their audience to new types of food.

Mukbangs originated on YouTube with Asian content creators and translates in English to *eating podcasts.* Although it started in 2010, this trend gained popularity with the rise of social media. The mukbang has branched out to many variations from when it first started. In 2015 Trisha Paytas, a popular YouTuber, exposed more American YouTube viewers to muckbangs. She began recording herself eating fast food and different restaurants. She helped expand the mukbang style video.

These videos are a new form of entertainment for many audiences. It may sound strange to watch someone eat on camera for hours, but it is actually not that uncommon. Many people watch as a source of entertainment. If viewers are interested in trying a new restaurant that has been included in a mukbang, they can get the full review of the food. They can also see foods that they have never thought of trying. Those who like watching mukbangs can even film their own mukbangs. All they need is food and a camera to record themselves and upload it for others. It can help the person recording the film not feel lonely while eating, and it can help the viewers to feel like they are eating with someone.

PRACTICE 1.3-C

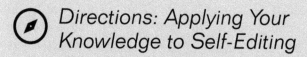

Directions: Applying Your Knowledge to Self-Editing

The purpose of this exercise is to add specificity, clarity, and interest to your writing with adverbials. Choose a text that you wrote before for this or another class. The text must be at least 300 words long. If you do not have a text of 300 words or more, you may choose to work with several shorter texts.

Add details to your own writing where necessary to show **when, where, how, why,** and **how often** (adverbials). Discuss your choices with a partner or small group.

NOTES

1 From: Urone, P. P., & Hinrichs, R. (2020). *College physics.* Rice University Open Stacks. Available for free at https://openstax.org/details/books/college-physics.

2 From: Urone, P. P., & Hinrichs, R. (2020). *College physics.* Rice University Open Stacks. Available for free at https://openstax.org/details/books/college-physics.

3 The sentences in this exercise have been adapted from the following sources:

Urone, P. P., & Hinrichs, R. (2020). *College physics.* Rice University Open Stacks. Available for free at https://openstax.org/details/books/college-physics.

Simic, Z., Havelka, J. G., & Vrhovcak, M. B. (2013). Small turbines – a unique segment of the wind power market. *Renewable Energy, 50,* 1027–1036.

Farrant, B. M., & Zubrick, S. R. (2013). Parent-child book reading across early childhood and child vocabulary in the early school years: Findings from the longitudinal study of Australian children. *First Language, 33*(3), 280–293.

Morse, H. (March 6, 2020). NEW: Coronavirus: 2 Florida patients die; 2 new cases in Broward County. *Palm Beach Daily News.* www.palmbeachdailynews.com/story/news/coronavirus/2020/03/06/new-coronavirus-2-florida-patients-die-2-new-cases-in-broward-county/112247732/. Retrieved from the Coronavirus Corpus: www.english-corpora.org/corona/.

Cain Miller, C. (2018, May 27). The number of women at the top is falling. *The New York Times,* Section BU, p. 4.

Business Insider, February 26, 2019. Retrieved from COCA. :www.english-corpora.org/coca/.

The Boston Globe, January 21, 2016. Retrieved from COCA: www.english-corpora.org/coca/

The Resilient Communities Blog. www.resilientcommunities.com/ive-got-a-unique-gift-for-long-time-readers/. Accessed on January 15, 2021.

⚠ 2
Using Effective Punctuation

Have you ever wondered if there are clear and straightforward rules for using punctuation? Of course, we all know that we must put a period, a question mark, or an exclamation point at the end of a sentence – depending on whether we are making a statement, asking a question, or expressing a strong emotion. That's elementary school stuff.

But what about commas? Or worse yet, semicolons? What are those for? Some of you may have heard – in middle or high school – that commas are used to indicate pauses, so if you read a sentence aloud and pause at some spot, that's a place to put a comma. You may also have been told that semicolons are just fancier and more formal versions of commas – they mark longer pauses and make you look all smart and sophisticated when you write.

But what if we told you that these "rules" are, actually, misconceptions? Well, they are.

And that is because writing – the only medium in which we use commas and semicolons – is not just speech captured in letters instead of sounds. When we speak, if our listeners do not understand something, we can immediately clarify, repeat, or reorganize our ideas right then and there to get our points across. When we write, however, our readers are not present. They cannot ask us to explain, repeat, or reword something if it is not clear right away. A writer must do their best from the outset to make sure that their ideas are logically presented and are easy to understand even for the reader who cannot ask questions every time something seems confusing.

This is where punctuation comes in. Proper punctuation (the use of commas, colons, and semicolons) helps writers establish the difference between main ideas and secondary ones. The text becomes more logical and readable when the writer enhances the structure of sentences and improves the flow from one sentence to another by using effective punctuation. Punctuation signposts for the reader

DOI: 10.4324/9781003159889-3

which ideas go together, and which ones need to be separated. It assists the writer in putting emphasis on the key details and concepts.

But most importantly, proper punctuation allows writers to amplify the power of their expression, to add a certain punch to their words, to elevate their credibility with the reader, and to gain their own voice that appeals directly to the audience and makes their writing persuasive and informative. By learning and using the fundamental rules of punctuation, you make yourself a stronger writer.

In this chapter you will:

- Become familiar with the most common principles and patterns of using commas in academic and professional writing
- Gain a fundamental understanding of less frequent punctuation marks – colons and semicolons
- Learn how to boost sentence variety in your writing
- Develop skills in editing your writing for proper punctuation

This chapter consists of five sections. In the first section, you will learn a few key terms that will help you think and talk about punctuation patterns in a simple, clear, and concise way. In the remaining sections, you will develop skills in successful use of punctuation in different sentence types.

2.1   Sentences and clauses
2.2   Sentences with equal clauses
2.3   Sentences with unequal clauses
        Subordination (adverbial and relative clauses)
        Embedding (subject and object clauses)
2.4   Introducing examples (sentences, clauses, phrases)
2.5   Sentence variety in academic and professional texts

Let's begin.

2.1 WHAT ARE THE DIFFERENT KINDS OF SENTENCES?

After you work through this section of the chapter, you will be well on the way to say confidently:

⊚ I can identify all subject-verb combinations in a sentence.

⊚ I understand what a clause is.

⊚ I can distinguish between single-clause and multi-clause sentences.

PRACTICE 2.1-A

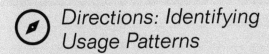

Directions: Identifying Usage Patterns

The purpose of this exercise is to draw your attention to the different numbers of subject-verb sets in sentences that occur in the types of texts you read and write in your classes.

- Read the passage below completely.
- For each underlined verb, find the corresponding subject.
- Fill in the table below the text to list the subject-verb combinations and to count the number of subject-verb combinations in each sentence.
- Sentences 1, 3, and 11 are done for you as examples.

From: Greenlaw, S. A., & Shapiro, D. (2018). *Principles of economics* (2nd ed.). Rice University Open Stax. Available for free at: https://d3bxy9euw4e147.cloudfront.net/oscms-prodcms/media/documents/Economics2e-OP_s2jF42u.pdf

(1) Economics <u>is concerned</u> with the well-being of all people, including those with jobs and those without jobs, as well as those with high incomes and those with low incomes. (2) Economics <u>acknowledges</u> that production of useful goods and services <u>can create</u> problems of environmental pollution. (3) It <u>explores</u> the question of how investing in education <u>helps</u> to develop workers' skills. (4) It <u>probes</u> questions like how to tell when big businesses or big labor unions <u>are operating</u> in a way that <u>benefits</u> society as a whole and when they <u>are operating</u> in a way that <u>benefits</u> their owners or members at the expense of others.

(5) It <u>looks</u> at how government spending, taxes, and regulations <u>affect</u> decisions about production and consumption.

(6) It <u>should be clear</u> by now that economics <u>covers</u> considerable ground. (7) We <u>can divide</u> that ground into two parts. (8) Microeconomics <u>focuses</u> on the actions of individual agents within the economy, like households, workers, and businesses. (9) Macroeconomics <u>looks</u> at the economy as a whole. (10) It <u>focuses</u> on broad issues such as growth of production, the number of unemployed people, the inflationary increase in prices, government deficits, and levels of exports and imports. (11) Microeconomics and macroeconomics <u>are not</u> separate subjects, but rather complementary perspectives on the overall subject of the economy.

	Subject-Verb Combinations	Number of Subject-Verb Combinations
(1)	<u>Economics is concerned</u>...	1
(2)		
(3)	<u>It explores</u>... ...<u>investing in education helps</u>...	2
(4)		
(5)		
(6)		
(7)		
(8)		
(9)		
(10)		
(11)	<u>Microeconomics and macroeconomics are not</u>	1

SUMMARY: SIMILARITIES AND DIFFERENCES BETWEEN SENTENCES AND CLAUSES

Clause	Sentence
A group of words that contains **one** subject-verb combination: • *Economics is concerned with the well-being of all people, including those with jobs and those without jobs, as well as those with high incomes and those with low incomes.* • *...that production of useful goods and services can create problems of environmental pollution.*	A group of words that contains **one or more** subject-verb combinations: • *Microeconomics focuses on the actions of individual agents within the economy, like households, workers, and businesses.* – One subject-verb combination. • *It explores the question of how investing in education helps to develop workers' skills.* – Two subject-verb combinations.
May or may not express a complete idea: • **Independent (complete idea; can be a sentence in itself)**: *Economics is concerned with the well-being of all people, including those with jobs and those without jobs, as well as those with high incomes and those with low incomes.* • **Dependent (incomplete idea; cannot be a sentence in itself)**: *... that economics covers considerable ground.*	Always expresses a complete idea: • *Microeconomics focuses on the actions of individual agents within the economy, like households, workers, and businesses.* • *It explores the question of how investing in education helps to develop workers' skills.*

PRACTICE 2.1-B

Directions: Identifying Clause Types

The purpose of this practice is to draw your attention to two aspects of sentence structure:

1. The number of clauses per sentence and
2. The kind of relationships clauses can have to one another within sentence.
    *   Read the text below carefully. All clauses in this text have been bracketed.
    *   In the right-hand column, list the number of clauses in each sentence.

- Then, mark each clause as a D for "dependent" or "I" for independent.
- Hint: To determine whether the clause is dependent or independent, read it aloud by itself, without thinking about how it connects to other clauses in the sentence. If it makes a complete idea, it's independent. If it makes only part of a complete idea, it is dependent.

From: Kraus, N., & White-Schwoch, T. (2020, July–August). The argument for music education. *American Scientist, 108*(4). www .americanscientist.org/article/the-argument-for-music-education.

Text	Clauses
I *I* (1) [Margaret Martin needed help]. (2) [It was early 2011 and had been 10 *D* years since she'd founded Harmony Project], [which provides free music lessons to children from underserved Los Angeles neighborhoods]. (3) [Martin made a simple deal with each student who enrolled]: (4) [if you maintained passing grades], [and if you attended every practice and performance at Harmony Project], [you would have a guaranteed spot for free] [until you graduated high school]. (5) [Demand for her program quickly outstripped the number of available openings], [and Martin grew desperate to shrink the waiting list].	(1) – 1 clause (2) – 2 clauses (3) (4) (5)
(6) [Harmony Project kept growing in popularity] [partly because its students excelled in not only music but also many seemingly unrelated areas]: (7) [They graduated at the top of their classes, earned college scholarships, and went on to successful careers]. (8) [Martin had touted those success stories] [as she tirelessly grew her project], [but now she needed school districts and large foundations to invest larger sums in Harmony Project]. (9) [She knew from her training in public health] [how to develop experimental data to convince policy makers].	(6) (7) (8) (9)
(10) [Martin saw] [that music was sparking something in her students' brains] [that was setting them up for academic success], [but she didn't have the evidence to prove it]. (11) [She realized] [that she needed the help of a neuroscientist].	(10) (11)

SUMMARY: TYPES OF SENTENCES

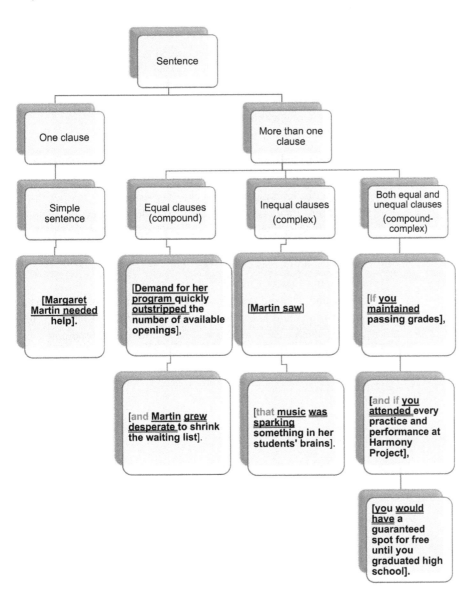

PRACTICE 2.1-C

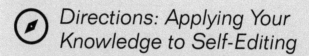

Directions: Applying Your Knowledge to Self-Editing

Now, it is your turn. Select a piece of your own writing about 300 words long. Identify all subject-verb combinations in it and bracket all the clauses. For every clause, decide whether it is an independent one or a dependent one within its sentence.

Discuss the following with a partner:

- How many clauses, on average, do your sentences tend to have?
- Do you have mostly simple sentences (the ones that have only one clause) or compound and complex sentences (the ones that have more than one clause each)? You do not need to try and identify which of these sentences are compound and which ones are complex.
- In your multi-clause sentences, are the clauses mostly equal, mostly unequal, or a mix of both?
- What kind of ideas do you tend to express in simple sentences? What about compound and complex sentences? Which sentences – in your opinion – carry more force, more power, more "oomph," so to say? Which ones, on the other hand, carry more information?

2.2 HOW DO I PUNCTUATE SENTENCES WITH EQUAL CLAUSES (COMPOUND SENTENCES)?

After you work through this section of the chapter, you will be well on the way to say confidently:

- ⦿ I can determine whether clauses in a sentence are equal or unequal to one another.

- ⦿ I can punctuate sentences with equal clauses linked by FANBOYS (coordinating conjunctions).

- ⦿ I can punctuate sentences with equal clauses **_not_** linked by FANBOYS.

PRACTICE 2.2-A

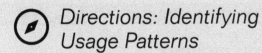

Directions: Identifying Usage Patterns

This exercise will lead you to discover punctuation patterns for sentences with two or more *equal clauses*. When two or more independent clauses are joined together, they create a compound sentence, where both (or all) clauses are equal in importance to the meaning and message of the whole sentence.

- Read the sentences from various publications below.
- Identify the clauses and commas in each sentence. You will find that each sentence contains two or more equal clauses.
- Answer the questions after the sentences to help you identify the patterns of using commas with sentences that have two or more equal clauses.
- Optional: Discuss the questions with a partner or small group.

1. Ronald Reagan made a lot of movies, and the Library makes it clear.
2. The GT4's hybrid powertrain is lighter than the gas engine, so engineers have added extra batteries to balance the craft's center of gravity.
3. The President may veto bills passed by Congress, but Congress may also override a veto by a two-thirds vote in both the Senate and the House of Representatives.

4. There's never going to be a shortage of jokes, nor will there ever be a shortage of hatred.

5. Home Improvement Retail earnings were pummeled by the housing recession in 2008, but analysts expect a return to double-digit earnings growth in 2010 and 2011.

6. Their preferred ideas of diseases are usually based in either prescientific concepts of human body functions and disease vectors, or they are based in completely unscientific belief systems.

7. The Latino population is slowing down in California, and it's growing in the rest of the United States.

8. The river had broken levees hundreds of miles upstream, so the flood crest never reached the city.

9. Since 2004, a larger number of earthquakes with magnitudes near 9.0 have been recorded, yet their frequency continues to fluctuate from year to year.

10. Abigail walked to the manor by herself, for she had learned the way there the day before.

Discussion Question	Answer
In these sentences with two or more equal clauses, which words connect one independent clause to another? List them here.	
Which punctuation should you use to join two or more equal clauses?	
Where should the punctuation be placed?	

PRACTICE 2.2-B

 Directions: Identifying Usage Patterns

Now that you have discovered the patterns of using the comma in sentences with equal clauses, let's look at the patterns of using the semicolon.

- Repeat the process of discovery you used in Practice 2.2-A.
- Read the sentences below.
- Identify all clauses in each sentence.

- Answer the questions after the sentences to help you identify the patterns of using semicolons with sentences that have two or more equal clauses.
- Optional: Discuss the questions with a partner or small group.[1]

1. Reliant believes the forward-looking statements contained herein are reasonable; however, many of such risks, uncertainties, and other factors are beyond Reliant's ability to control or predict.
2. Teaching through Zoom has resulted in a decrease in learning ability in a significant number of children; many children experienced mental distress and hunger.
3. The process of refining admissions criteria should be continual; improvement is always possible.
4. Vibhath Jayasinghe is one of the first two President Scouts in the history of Royal Institute; moreover, he is a gifted actor, dancer, and a stage director.
5. They are not adversaries; on the contrary, they work together to build coalitions and share power.
6. Despite a shift in priorities last year, the company stayed committed to CSR (Corporate Social Responsibility) and stepped it up in the area of social justice; as a matter of fact, social justice is front and center with Cisco leadership.

Discussion Question	Answer
Are there specific words that connect independent clauses in the sentences above? What are they? Are these words always present?	
Which punctuation should you use to join two or more equal clauses?	
Where should the punctuation be placed?	
If the second clause has an introductory word or phrase at its beginning, which punctuation mark comes after this word?	

SUMMARY: PUNCTUATING SENTENCES WITH EQUAL CLAUSES (COMPOUND SENTENCES)

Connecting Words	Punctuation Patterns	Examples	Grammatical Term
FANBOYS: • For • And • Nor • But • Or • Yet • So	Put a comma **before** one of the FANBOYS (when it is followed by a subject and verb)	2020 was a year like no other in our lifetime, **and** the world was looking for someone to step up and help us navigate these challenging times. There is too much to cover from the 150-page report in one post, **but** the company is making strides in driving inclusiveness.	Coordinating conjunctions
• However, • moreover, • on the contrary, • on the other hand, • consequently, • as a result, • (etc.)	Put a semicolon at the end of the first clause. Put a comma after the connecting word. If the connecting word is in the middle of the second clause, put commas on both sides of it.	Observational studies provide important insights into human behavior; **however,** their results cannot be generalized beyond specific sites and populations. The number of women in the engineering profession is growing steadily; **still,** challenges remain in this highly male-dominated field. When 1960s activists used nonviolent civil disobedience, law enforcement responded with violence; **as a result,** public support, moral authority and control of the narrative shifted from the state to the activists.	Conjunctive adverbials; logical connectors
No connecting word	Put a semicolon after the first clause.	By the 18th century, alcohol consumption was part and parcel of daily life; it was served at nearly every meal.	Semicolon

EDITING STRATEGIES

Problem	Example	How to correct
Two or more equal clauses are separated by a comma without one of the FANBOYS Term: Comma splice	One very important aspect of hotel management is in hotel design, the ability to predict and provide for customer needs is crucial to it.	Identify the clause boundaries. *[One very important aspect of hotel management is in hotel design], [the ability to predict and provide for customer needs is crucial to it].* **Option 1:** Add one of the FANBOYS. This option has a smooth flow for the reader and emphasizes the close relationship between the ideas in each clause: *[One very important aspect of hotel management is in hotel design], **and** [the ability to predict and provide for customer needs is crucial to it].* **Option 2:** Change the comma to a semicolon. This option separates the ideas, but indicates to the reader to notice the relationship between the ideas in the two clauses: *[One very important aspect of hotel management is in hotel design]; [the ability to predict and provide for customer needs is crucial to hotel design].* **Option 3:** Split the sentence into two with a period. This option separates the two ideas. Each sentence has more individual emphasis; however, it may lead to a choppy style: *One very important aspect of hotel management is in hotel design. The ability to predict and provide for customer needs is crucial to it.*

(Continued)

Problem	Example	How to correct
Two or more clauses are joined without any punctuation – i.e., run together. Term: Run-on or fused sentence	*The very definition of a driver's license is freedom every teen dreams of getting their driver's license and going anywhere they want to go.*	Identify the clause boundaries. *[The very definition of a driver's license is freedom] [every teen dreams of getting their driver's license and going anywhere they want to go].* **Option 1:** Add a comma and one of the FANBOYS in between the two clauses. This option has a smooth flow for the reader and emphasizes the close relationship between the ideas in each clause: *[The very definition of a driver's license is freedom],* **so** *[every teen dreams of getting their driver's license and going anywhere they want to go].* **Option 2:** Separate the clauses with a semicolon. Connecting words are optional. This option separates the ideas, but indicates to the reader to notice the relationship between the ideas in the two clauses: *[The very definition of a driver's license is freedom]; [every teen dreams of getting their driver's license and going anywhere they want to go].* *[The very definition of a driver's license is freedom]; therefore, [every teen dreams of getting their driver's license and going anywhere they want to go].* **Option 3:** Put a period between the clauses and start the second sentence with a capital letter. This option separates the two ideas. Each sentence has more individual emphasis; however, it may lead to a choppy style: *[The very definition of a driver's license is freedom]. [Every teen dreams of getting their driver's license and going anywhere they want to go].*

PRACTICE 2.2-C

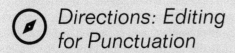

Directions: Editing for Punctuation

The goal of this exercise is to help you apply what you have learned about punctuating sentences with equal clauses. You will practice your skills in editing a text for punctuation. The passage below is an excerpt from a student research paper. Read it carefully and edit it for punctuation, following these steps:

- Read through the whole text once without focusing on grammar or punctuation first. You need to do this to get the general idea of the text's meaning and direction.
- Then, read through the text again and identify all subject-verb phrase combinations.
- Mark all clause boundaries.
- Where the clauses in a sentence are equal, determine whether the punctuation patterns are applied appropriately. Some sentences will have correct punctuation, and some will not, but the punctuation errors will be found only in sentences with equal clauses.
- If punctuation needs correction, choose one of the strategies from the table above to correct it. Remember: there is no one single way to correct every punctuation problem – you have several choices in each case.
- Optional: Discuss these choices with a partner or group. How does choosing one pattern over another affect the flow of the text? Which ones do you think will work better for this flow than others? Why?

Chemical Engineering and Cosmetics

The interest of people in their physical appearance started a long time ago, however, it is becoming more and more important today. Our body lets us express our feelings and thoughts. More importantly, the way we see ourselves affects the way others see us and interact with us, choosing respect or indifference. Vesilind (2008) reports that 80% of women are unhappy with their appearance and the correlation between physical appearance and self-confidence is a significant issue today. Moreover, this problem is becoming a growing trend that affects teenagers as well as adults.

In America and in many countries in the world, the media presents us with models of beauty, which leads to a decrease in girls' and women's confidence as they attempt to compare themselves to this definition of beauty. The media images are really important in our life, we cannot ignore them, even if they do present women as perfect as Barbie dolls. A study demonstrated that the media does not express the societal perception of the body; but it does shape a perfect and ideal image of women (Turner et al., 1997, 603–14). We are not only constantly bombarded with these images; we are also subjected to the pressure to look like these models.

Since many people admit they feel bad and insecure about themselves because of their physical appearance, cosmetics seem to be the best solution to both improve their self-image and to give them the ability to face other peoples' opinions with much more confidence. Thanks to cosmetics, which give them the power to change their appearance, women can have a better image of themselves.

PRACTICE 2.2-D

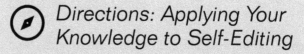

Directions: Applying Your Knowledge to Self-Editing

Now, it's your turn. Choose a passage from your own writing about 300 words long. Using the same strategies as in Practice 2.2-C above, edit it for punctuation in sentences with equal clauses.

After you complete the editing process, reflect on the following:

- Did you find any errors you needed to correct?
- If yes, what types of punctuation errors were they: comma splices or run-on sentences?
- In examining your original punctuation errors and subsequent corrections, do you see any patterns? Are there particular punctuation problems that seem to be more common for you in your writing? How will you make sure that you make fewer such errors in the future or avoid them altogether?

2.3 HOW DO I PUNCTUATE SENTENCES WITH UNEQUAL CLAUSES (COMPLEX SENTENCES)?

After you work through this section, you will be well on the way to say confidently:

◎ I can identify unequal (dependent) clauses in a multi-clause sentence.

◎ I understand the different jobs dependent clauses do in a multi-clause sentence.

◎ I can properly punctuate sentences with dependent clauses.

PRACTICE 2.3-A

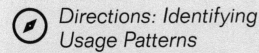

Directions: Identifying Usage Patterns

The purpose of this exercise is to draw your attention to what kinds of jobs dependent clauses do in multi-clause sentences and what kind of information they convey. In the left-hand column, you have an original text from the website of the National Park Service Ethnography Program (www.nps.gov/ethnography/contact.htm). The text is an introduction to the description of medieval African civilizations. The dependent clauses in the passage have been underlined and boldfaced. On the right, you have the same text somewhat modified – the dependent clauses have been replaced with phrases or converted into separate sentences. Think back to what you learned about sentence elements in Chapter 2 and then decide what kind of job each clause and phrase does in the sentence, i.e., what kind of sentence element it is in the multi-clause sentence. Then mark this job in the right-most column. Here some of the jobs these clauses do that you may want to consider:

- Tells **time, place**, or **manner of action** (adverbial)
- Refers to the **subject** of the sentence (subject)
- Tells us what the **object** of the action is: What did the subject tell, think, know, etc.? (object)
- **Describes** a person, thing, or phenomenon (adjective)
- Provides **additional but not essential information** about something (additional info)

Sentences 1, 3, and 5(b) have been marked as examples.

From: Park Ethnography Program. **Provided by:** National Park Service. **Located at:** www.nps.gov/ethnography/aah/aaheritage /histContextsA.htm. **Project:** African American Heritage and Ethnography. **License:** *Public Domain: No Known Copyright*

Original Text	Modified Text	Job of the dependent clause
(1) <u>When the Portuguese first explored the West African coastline</u>, the cultures of African societies were highly evolved and had been so for centuries. (2) In the millennium preceding Portuguese exploration, three large centers of medieval African civilization developed sequentially along the west coast of sub-Saharan Africa. (3) The first polity <u>that is known to have gained prominence</u> was Ancient Ghana. (4) Between 500 AD–1250 AD, Ancient Ghana flourished in the southern Sahel north of the middle Niger and middle Senegal Rivers. (5) Boahen (1966) bases his account of Ancient Ghana on Al-Bakri and Al-Idrisi, two Arabic scholars writing their descriptions in 1067 and in 1154 respectively, <u>when Ghana was at the height of its power.</u> (6) He tells us <u>that Ancient Ghana had a civil service, strong monarchy based on a matrilineal system of inheritance, a cabinet, an army, an effective justice system and a regular source of income from trade as well as tribute from vassal kings</u> (Boahen, 1966:4–9).	(1) <u>During the initial exploration of the African West Coast by the Portuguese</u>, the cultures of African societies were highly evolved and had been so for centuries. (2) In the millennium preceding Portuguese exploration, three large centers of medieval African civilization developed sequentially along the west coast of sub-Saharan Africa. (3) The first **prominent** polity was Ancient Ghana. (4) Between 500 AD–1250 AD, Ancient Ghana flourished in the southern Sahel north of the middle Niger and middle Senegal Rivers. (5a) Boahen (1966) bases his account of Ancient Ghana on Al-Bakri and Al-Idrisi, two Arabic scholars writing their descriptions in 1067 and in 1154 respectively. (5b) <u>It was the time of Ghana's height of power.</u> (6) He tells us <u>the story of</u> Ancient <u>Ghana's civil service, strong monarchy based on a matrilineal system of inheritance, a cabinet, an army, an effective justice system, and a regular source of income from trade as well as tribute from vassal kings</u> (Boahen, 1966:4–9). (7) <u>In the</u>	(1) Tells time (adverbial) (3) Describes the word *polity* (adjective) (5b) Additional info about the years 1067–1154. (6) (7)

(Continued)

Original Text	Modified Text	Job of the dependent clause
(7) <u>As Ghana declined over the next 200 years</u>, the ancient Mali Empire arose in the same area but descended territorially further along the Niger River. (8) Mali encompassed a huge area stretching from the Lower Senegal and Upper Niger rivers eastward to the Niger bend and northward to the Sahel. (9) Its great size made Mali an even more diverse state than Ghana. (10) The majority of the people lived in small villages and cultivated rice or sorghums and millets, <u>**while some communities specialized in herding and fishing.**</u> (11) Trade flourished in the towns, <u>**which housed a wide array of craftspeople** along with a growing number of Islamic teachers and holy men</u>. (12) The main commercial centers were its capitals Niani, Timbuktu, and Gao.	<u>course of Ghana's decline over the next 200 years</u>, the ancient Mali Empire arose in the same area but descended territorially further along the Niger River. (8) Mali encompassed a huge area stretching from the Lower Senegal and Upper Niger rivers eastward to the Niger bend and northward to the Sahel. (9) Its great size made Mali an even more diverse state than Ghana. (10a) The majority of the people lived in small villages and cultivated rice or sorghums and millets. (10b) <u>**At the same time, some communities specialized in herding and fishing.**</u> (11a) Trade flourished in the towns. (11b) <u>**These towns housed a wide array of craftspeople** along with a growing number of Islamic teachers and holy men</u>. (12) The main commercial centers were its capitals Niani, Timbuktu, and Gao.	(10b) (11)

🏃 SUMMARY: TYPES OF UNEQUAL/ DEPENDENT CLAUSES (COMPLEX SENTENCES)

What It Does	Example	Grammatical Term
Tells the time, place, manner, condition, or reason of the action in the full sentence	<u>When the Portuguese first explored the West African coastline</u>, the cultures of African societies were highly evolved and had been so for centuries. (time)	Adverb clause
	It was early 2011 and had been 10 years <u>since Margaret Martin had founded Harmony Project</u>. (starting point in time)	
	Harmony Project kept growing in popularity <u>partly because its students excelled in not only music but also many seemingly unrelated areas</u>. (reason)	
	<u>If you maintained passing grades</u>, and <u>if you attended every practice and performance at Harmony Project</u>, you would have a guaranteed spot for free <u>until you graduated high school</u>. (condition; condition; time)	
Completes the verb and tells what the subject thinks, feels, knows, sees, asks, etc.	The survey finds <u>that Americans have broad exposure to guns</u>, whether they personally own one or not.	Object clause
	Economics acknowledges <u>that production of useful goods and services can create problems of environmental pollution</u>.	
	When *Popular Mechanics* inquired <u>how the Air Force trained these elite troops</u>, we were invited to take a closer look for ourselves by observing them in action.	
	The research aimed to find out <u>if teachers with higher reflective skills demonstrate higher quality in their teaching performance</u>.	
Stands in place of the subject of the sentence	<u>What we would like to know</u> is how to test each variant safely.	Subject clause
	<u>That the tactic of occupation was the most effective form of protest</u> was obvious to all observers.	

(Continued)

What It Does	Example	Grammatical Term
Refers back to the subject *it*	<u>It</u> was obvious to all observers **that the tactic of occupation was the most effective term of protest**. <u>It</u> appears **that some of the animal mummies with applique designs may have been displayed**.	Transposed subject clause
Describes or defines a common noun	Moreover, this problem is becoming a growing *trend* **that affects teenagers as well as adults**. Apprenticeship is a *system* **which is predicated on a training agreement between an apprentice and a mentor or trainer**. Only 46% of *students* **who enter community college with a specific goal in mind**, such as earning a credential or transferring to a 4-year university, actually complete this goal or are still enrolled 6 years later.	Relative clause (aka adjective clause)
Provides supplemental and non-essential information or elaborates and comments on already-stated information.	It was early 2011 and had been 10 years since she'd founded Harmony Project, **which provides free music lessons to children from underserved Los Angeles neighborhoods**. (Additional info about the unique Harmony Project.) Boahen (1966) bases his account of Ancient Ghana on Al-Bakri and Al-Idrisi, two Arabic scholars writing their descriptions in 1067 and in 1154 respectively, **when Ghana was at the height of its power**. (Elaborates on why writing descriptions of Ghana between 1067 and 1154 is important.) In America and in many countries in the world, the media presents us with models of beauty, **which leads to a decrease in girls' and women's confidence as they attempt to compare themselves to this definition of beauty**. (Comments on what the presentation of models of beauty does for women's confidence.)	Elaboration or comment clause

PRACTICE 2.3-B

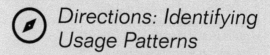

Directions: Identifying Usage Patterns

In this exercise, you will practice identifying different types of dependent clauses in an excerpt from a student opinion essay. The writer of this passage skillfully used a variety of dependent clauses to convey their idea in a crisp and clear way. The writer also correctly punctuated all the sentences with dependent clauses.

- Read through the passage once to get its general idea.
- The dependent clauses in the passage have been identified and underlined. Examine each dependent clause and decide whether it is an **adverb clause**, a **subject clause**, an **object clause**, an **adjective clause**, or an **elaboration/comment clause**.
- Fill in the table below.

In the year 2008, according to a survey done by the Fatality Analysis Reporting System, there were 26,689 fatalities due to car collisions in the United States. In an age with constant technological improvements, not being able to reduce those numbers in one of the most technologically advanced countries is a shame. **While we make constant improvements in our vehicles' mileage and velocity**, we have not made enough improvements in the protection for the people **who ride in the vehicles**. **While many companies boast about their cars receiving awards for safety**, the number of fatalities in motor vehicle accidents has been reduced by only a few thousand in the past decade and half.

Motor vehicle companies have made astonishing improvements in motor vehicles, from cars to motorcycles, to make them faster and more efficient, but along with those improvements, we also need to improve safety for the vehicles at an even faster rate. **When you give cars the ability to easily reach 100mph**, people will go that fast **if they only can**. With that understanding in mind, we need to make sure **that motor vehicles can withstand collisions well enough so that the passengers and drivers can survive with as few injuries as possible**.

Car companies have put safety as a second priority many times in the past, and they, unfortunately, still continue to do so sometimes. The companies make their engineers concentrate on saving as much money as possible. They only care about their customers' safety **because they are afraid of being sued**. In the past, the car companies have skimmed on the quality of the components **that are needed for the vehicle's absolute safety**, **which has cost people lives**.

To sell cars, motor vehicle companies have put their interest in the fuel efficiency. **Although they do not ignore safety**, they may not be doing enough to make motor vehicles safe enough compared to the other technologies **that have been advancing rapidly**. **What mechanical engineers do** is work on the improvement of vehicle safety from year to year. This is the reason **that cars nowadays can withstand collisions much better than in the past decades**. **But even though engineers are improving vehicles**, cars have a long way to go **before they are 100% safe**.

Clause Type	Clauses from the Text
Adverb clauses	While we make constant improvements in our vehicles' mileage and velocity,
Object clauses	
Subject clauses or transposed subject clauses	
Adjective clauses	who ride in the vehicles
Elaboration/ Comment clauses	

PRACTICE 2.3-C

 Directions: Discovering the Rules of Punctuation

In this exercise, you will focus on discovering the rules of punctuation for dependent clauses.

- Go back to the student text in Practice 2.3-B.
- Examine the punctuation around each dependent clause. Observe the patterns and consistencies.
- Then complete the guidelines for punctuation based on your observations.
- Using the guidelines you came up with, edit the student passage below for proper punctuation of dependent clauses.

Guidelines:

1. If an adverb clause comes before the main (independent) clause, <u>put a comma after the adverb clause</u>

2. If an adverb clause comes after the main (independent) clause,

3. An adjective clause must come immediately after the noun it describes. There is

4. A subject **or** object clause cannot

5. A comment or elaboration clause is always

Passage for Editing:

Blood Transfusion

Many people believe, that blood transfusion is the best and the most common way to treat blood diseases such as hemophilia and sickle-cell as well as to save peoples' lives from trauma due to accidents. The ability to transfuse blood or its components to patients has revolutionized medical care, since it was invented. There were many trials, that were performed in the seventeenth century, but all of them failed because of the lack of technology and lack of proper knowledge. The first successful blood transfusion surgery was not completed until the nineteenth century.

There are many positive sides to blood transfusion, but at the same time there are some negative effects as well. One of the viruses, that is well-known and can cause infection from coming in contact with a needle from blood transfusion, is called Human Immunodeficiency Virus (HIV). But the rate of infection is really low today, because blood is tested for the viruses and other diseases before transfusion. Blood type can be a problem too. If the blood type doesn't fit the patient's type there will be a chance that the patient's body will reject it. But it is also extremely rare today, because hospitals or clinics check blood type before infusion. Before transfusion, doctors mix the samples of the patient's blood and the donor's blood to check for a harmful reaction which is called a cross-match test.

SUMMARY: PUNCTUATING SENTENCES WITH UNEQUAL CLAUSES (COMPLEX SENTENCES)

Clause Type	Punctuation Pattern	Examples
Adverb clauses: Tell time, place, manner, condition, reason, purpose, etc. of the action in the main clause	Put a comma after the adverb clause if the adverb clause precedes the main clause.	**Before school begins,** the band teacher should send a letter to the parents of all registered beginning band students.
	Don't use a comma before the adverb clause if it follows the main clause.	Teachers and librarians have concluded that the best system for developing a strong reading program is to block out time together **before school begins**.
	The comma is optional but recommended if the adverb clause also serves as an elaboration or comment on the main clause. Such comments or elaborations are usually not essential to the meaning of the whole sentence.	The unemployment situation is slowly improving, **although we must consider these latest figures with a degree of caution**.
Subject, object, or transposed subject clauses: Take up the place of an essential element in the sentence structure	Do not separate any "noun" clauses – i.e., subject clauses, transposed subject clauses that refer back to the word *it* at the beginning of the sentence, or object clauses – from the rest of the sentence by any punctuation marks.	Margaret Martin knew from her training in public health **how to develop experimental data to convince policy makers**. (Object of the verb *knew*)
		Teachers and librarians have concluded **that the best system is to block out time together at the beginning of the school year**. (Object of the verb *concluded*)
		It appears **that social capital has a positive effect on mental health**. (Transposed clause referring to the word *it*).
		What became patently obvious on my second trip to the city was that the air quality had worsened significantly since my first visit. (Subject of the verb *was*).

(Continued)

Clause Type	Punctuation Pattern	Examples
Adjective (relative) clauses: Provide important or essential information about the noun they describe	Do not use commas to separate these adjective-like (relative) clauses from the noun they describe	It probes questions like how to tell when big businesses or big labor unions are operating in *a way* <u>that benefits society as a whole</u> and when they are operating in *a way* <u>that benefits their owners or members at the expense of others</u>. A writer must do their best from the outset to make sure that their ideas are logically presented and are easy to understand even for *the reader* <u>who cannot ask questions every time something seems confusing</u>.
Elaboration, additional non-essential information, and comment clauses: Provide "by the way" information – something that may be an afterthought or not entirely necessary to the meaning and structure of the whole sentence but is interesting to add.	Always separate elaboration clauses from the rest of the sentence by commas.	In America and in many countries in the world, the media presents us with models of beauty, <u>which leads to a decrease in girls' and women's confidence as they attempt to compare themselves to this definition of beauty</u>. Thanks to *cosmetics*<u>, which give them the power to change their appearance,</u> women can have a better image of themselves. Boahen (1966) bases his account of Ancient Ghana on Al-Bakri and Al-Idrisi, two Arabic scholars writing their descriptions *in 1067 and in 1154 respectively*, <u>when Ghana was at the height of its power</u>.

PRACTICE 2.3-D

 Directions: Applying Your Knowledge to Self-Editing

It is time to apply the editing tips to your own writing. Choose a passage from your own writing about 300 words long. Read the passage once through to remind yourself of the content and main idea. Then, identify all dependent clauses in it. Examine the punctuation and make corrections where necessary. After you complete the editing process, reflect on the following:

- Did you find any errors you needed to correct?
- If yes, what types of punctuation errors were they? Did you tend to omit commas where they were necessary or insert unneeded commas?
- In examining your original punctuation errors and subsequent corrections, do you see any patterns? Are there particular punctuation problems that seem to be more common for you in your writing? How will you make sure that you make fewer such errors in the future or avoid them altogether?

2.4 HOW DO I USE PUNCTUATION TO CLARIFY OR INTRODUCE EXAMPLES?

After you work through this section of the chapter, you will be well on the way to say confidently:

◎ I can identify supporting details and examples in a sentence.

◎ I can identify examples that are complete sentences as opposed to nouns, lists of nouns, -ing words, or dependent clauses.

◎ I can properly punctuate sentences with examples or clarifying ideas.

 SUMMARY: INTRODUCING AND PUNCTUATING EXAMPLES AND CLARIFICATIONS

Meaning	Introductory Term and/or Punctuation	Placement and Usage	Examples
Some supporting details for the word directly mentioned before	such as	[Word referring to a general category], **such as** a noun, list of nouns, -ing word(s), or dependent clause.* *If the example comes in the middle of the complete sentence, you should also include a comma at the end of your example(s).	Cruciferous vegetables<u>, such as</u> cauliflower, have anti-cancer properties.
	like	[Word referring to a general category], **like** a noun, list of nouns, -ing word(s), or dependent clause.*	Vitamin C is found in colorful vegetables<u>, like</u> bell peppers.

(Continued)

Meaning	Introductory Term and/or Punctuation	Placement and Usage	Examples
	e.g. (The Latin term *exempli gratia* is abbreviated to e.g.)	[Word referring to a general category], **e.g.**, a noun, list of nouns, -ing word(s), or dependent clause.*	Green leafy vegetables, **e.g.**, spinach, contain calcium.
	for example	[Word referring to a general category], **for example**, a noun, list of nouns, -ing word(s), or dependent clause.* **For example**, [complete sentence].** **The introductory words can also come after the subject with a comma before and after.	Calcium is found in green leafy vegetables, **for example**, kale, arugula, and spinach. Calcium is found in green leafy vegetables. **For example**, kale, arugula, and spinach have over 160 mg. per serving.
	for instance	[Complete sentence], **for instance**, a noun, list of nouns, -ing word(s), or dependent clause.* **For instance**, [complete sentence].**	Vitamin C is found in colorful vegetables. Red bell peppers, **for instance**, have a lot of vitamin C.
All of the examples for the word directly mentioned before or saying specifically what you mentioned previously	namely	[Word referring to a category], **namely** a noun, list of nouns, -ing word(s), or dependent clause. (Note: Stylistically, a comma is sometimes used after *namely*.)	Vitamin D is only found in one plant source, **namely** mushrooms.

(Continued)

Meaning	Introductory Term and/or Punctuation	Placement and Usage	Examples
	i.e. (The Latin term *id est* is abbreviated to i.e.)	[Word referring to a general category], **i.e.,** a noun, list of nouns, -ing word(s), or dependent clause.*	Anti-cancer properties are found in leafy cruciferous vegetables, **i.e.,** arugula, collard greens, cress, bok choy, cabbage, Brussels sprouts, kale, mustard greens, and turnip greens.
	: (a colon)	[Word referring to a general category]: a noun, list of nouns, -ing word(s), or dependent clause. [Complete sentence containing the word you are exemplifying]: [complete sentence].	Vitamin D is only found in one plant source: mushrooms. One simple change will add a lot of vital nutrients to your diet: eat more vegetables.

PRACTICE 2.4-A

 Directions: Applying Your Knowledge to Your Own Writing

Choose a topic that you are writing about for an assignment in progress. Write a sentence with your own ideas on your topic to introduce examples for each introductory term and/or punctuation below. Write a different sentence each time; do not just repeat the same sentence. Use the information above to help you use correct punctuation.

1. like
2. such as
3. for example (in the middle of a sentence)
4. for instance (in the middle of a sentence)
5. e.g.
6. For example (at the beginning of a new sentence)
7. For instance (at the beginning of a new sentence)
8. namely
9. i.e.
10. : (a colon)

2.5 HOW DO I VARY MY SENTENCE TYPES IN ACADEMIC AND PROFESSIONAL WRITING?

After you work through this section, you will be well on the way to say confidently:

◎ I understand the purpose of varying sentence structure in writing.

◎ I can combine or separate sentences effectively in my own writing to achieve clarity, directness, and coherence.

PRACTICE 2.5-A

 Directions: Identifying Usage Patterns

The purpose of this exercise is to bring your attention to how writers use dependent and independent clauses to create clear and polished sentences that flow smoothly and convey the writer's ideas in a logical and sophisticated way.

- Read the passage from a college physics textbook below.
- With a partner, identify all sentences that have two or more clauses and determine whether the clauses are equal or unequal. The first two sentences have been marked as examples.
- Discuss the following:
    - Why might the authors have chosen to start and end the sentences the way they did?
    - Why might they have chosen to combine equal clauses? Why might they have chosen unequal clauses?
    - Is there a difference in the flow of writing between sentences beginning with a dependent clause and sentences ending in a dependent clause?
    - Are there other choices in clause combination the authors may have made? What are they? How would the meaning or flow of the text be different if they had?

From: Urone, P. P., & Hinrichs, R. (2020). *College physics.* Rice University Open Stacks. Available for free at https://openstax.org/details/books/college-physics.

(1) [A model is a representation of something] [that is often too difficult (or impossible) to display directly]. (2) [While a model is justified with experimental proof,] [it is only accurate under limited situations.] (3) An example is the planetary model of the atom, in which electrons are pictured as orbiting the nucleus, analogous to the way planets orbit the Sun. (4) We cannot observe electron orbits directly, but the mental image helps explain the observations we can make, such as the emission of light from hot gases (atomic spectra). (4) Physicists use models for a variety of purposes. (5) For example, models can help physicists analyze a scenario and perform a calculation, or they can be used to represent a situation in the form of a computer simulation. (6) A theory is an explanation for patterns in nature that is supported by scientific evidence and verified multiple times by various groups of researchers. (7) Some theories include models to help visualize phenomena, whereas others do not. (8) Newton's theory of gravity, for example, does not require a model or mental image because we can observe the objects directly with our own senses. (9) The kinetic theory of gases, on the other hand, is a model in which a gas is viewed as being composed of atoms and molecules. (10) Atoms and molecules are too small to be observed directly with our senses—thus, we picture them mentally to understand what our instruments tell us about the behavior of gases.

(1) Unequal clauses

(2) Unequal clauses

SUMMARY: COMBINING OR SEPARATING IDEAS

Reason to Combine/ Separate	Examples
Add ideas	<u>Idea 1</u>: Ms. Martin saw that music was sparking something in her students' brains that was setting them up for academic success. <u>Idea 2</u>: She didn't have the evidence to prove it. <u>Combining ideas for a smooth flow</u>: Ms. Martin saw that music was sparking something in her students' brains that was setting them up for academic success, **but** she didn't have the evidence to prove it.
Specify details	<u>Idea 1</u>: We speak. <u>Idea 2</u>: Our listeners do not understand something. <u>Idea 3</u>: We can immediately clarify, repeat, or reorganize our ideas right then and there in order to get our points across. <u>Combining ideas for coherence</u>: When we speak, if our listeners do not understand something, we can immediately clarify, repeat, or reorganize our ideas right then and there in order to get our points across.
Describe or comment	<u>Idea 1</u>: This problem is becoming a growing trend. <u>Idea 2</u>: The trend affects teenagers as well as adults. <u>Combining ideas for clarity</u>: This problem is becoming a growing trend that affects teenagers as well as adults.
Increase precision and clarity	<u>Multiple complex ideas in one sentence</u>: When accountants make decisions, they must consider two types of users, which are external users, such as investors, stockholders, or creditors, who are the people who put their money into the company, and internal users, such as management and workers, who circulate inside the company and keep it going. <u>Separating ideas for clarity</u>: When accountants make decisions, they must consider two types of users: external ones and internal ones. External users are people who put money into the company. They include investors, stockholders, and creditors. Internal users are management and workers. They circulate inside the company and keep it going.

Revision Strategies: Combining Ideas

When you revise individual simple sentences in order to combine ideas, you have several options. As a writer, you have the control of which option will work better for your text flow.

Example:
Dentists give people anesthetics. An anesthetic is a drug or an herb. It is used to cause anesthesia. Anesthesia is a loss of sensation.

Option 1: Turn some of ideas into dependent clauses:
<u>When people go to the dentist</u>, they often get an anesthetic, <u>which is a drug or an herb</u> <u>that causes the loss of sensation</u>.

Option 2: Turn one of the ideas into an -ing phrase, a to-verb phrase, or an -ed phrase

An anesthetic is a drug or an herb <u>used to cause the loss of painful sensation</u>.

An anesthetic is a drug or an herb <u>causing the loss of pain sensation</u>.

Example:
In ancient times, pharmaceutical anesthetics did not exist. People used herbs and leaves to reduce pain.

Option 3: Combine simple sentences into a clause with parallel and equal ideas:

In ancient times, pharmaceutical anesthetics did not exist, <u>so people used herbs and leaves to reduce pain.</u>

PRACTICE 2.5-B

 Directions: Revision Choices in Practice

In this exercise, you will practice revising excerpts from papers written by students just like you.

- Work with a partner.
- Discuss each short passage from student writing below and decide whether you want to combine ideas in them or separate them for better flow and clarity.
- Then, make revisions by applying the strategies discussed above. Make sure to punctuate the revised versions properly.
- Remember: because different writers may make different stylistic choices, there is no one correct answer to each passage. Your answers will vary.
- Share your suggestions for revisions with others in class.

1. Safety is always the main concern of engineers. Especially in designing airplanes. There is a reason for that. In case of failure, the consequences will be terrible. There have not been many cases of airplane crashes. There have been enough to consider it a problem.

    _____
    _____
    _____
    _____
    _____
    _____

2. Most organisms on this planet, if not all of them, need some component which the air contains on this planet in order to survive, even though we do get these components, such as oxygen for humans, the air which we breathe also contaminates us and inserts toxic waste into our bodies with every breath we take.

    _____
    _____
    _____
    _____
    _____
    _____

3. Since its peak in 2000, the music industry has been suffering from a severe recession. The demand for the music download services is growing. Because of that, CD sales today show a decline. In 2010, the sales dropped by 50% compared to 2000. Trends are rapidly changing with the times. The entire music industry has not invented a practical gimmick to help CD sales yet. Maybe the CDs will disappear completely in the future.

    _____
    _____
    _____
    _____
    _____
    _____

4. During the beginning of the 19th century President Jefferson proposed the public school system. In this century only the wealthy children could attend schools. By the end of the century all children were required to attend at least elementary school. The children of color were allowed to attend public school during Lincoln's presidency. By the 20th century all children were required to attend high school either private or public. Today there are over 15,000 school districts.

_____

_____

_____

_____

_____

PRACTICE 2.5-C

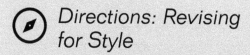

Directions: Revising for Style

In this practice, you will exercise all the choices of weaving a complete text out of fluid, sophisticated, clear, and informative sentences.

- Read the passage below. This passage was written by an 8th grader. It is informative, but its style is choppy and still immature, as one would expect of an 8th grader.
- Work with a partner to revise this text. You must retain all the information in it, but at the same time create a more polished style and flow by combining simple ideas into more complex sentences.
- There is no one correct answer to this task. After completing it, compare your newly created passage with the passages created by other groups. Discuss the differences and advantages and disadvantages of particular grammatical choices.

Why Save Energy?

Many people and organizations talk about saving energy these days. This is called the Green Movement. This movement empowers people to become eco-friendly and protect our planet. There are many reasons to go green and save energy. First, reducing energy use decreases the amount of greenhouse gases in the atmosphere. The greenhouse gases are, to a great degree, responsible for the current climate change. The planet is getting hotter and hotter every year. This temperature increase causes icecaps to melt. It also leads to many natural disasters, such as hurricanes and floods. Fewer greenhouse gases mean fewer extreme weather events: draughts, deadly blizzards, and devastating tornadoes. Second, reducing energy use improves the quality of life. The air and the water remain clean. People suffer less from such illnesses as asthma and allergies. Animals can live in their natural habitats. The agricultural industry, unharmed by severe weather, continues to grow food sufficient for all people. The general standard of living continues to increase across the world. The third, and most practical reason to save energy is money. Reducing energy use brings down your utility bills. You can save a lot of money on your electricity, water, and gas every year. Do you want to do your part? Join the Green Movement, save money, and save the planet for the future generations.

PRACTICE 2.5-D

 Directions: Applying Your Knowledge to Self-Editing

It is time to apply sentence editing strategies to your own writing. Choose a passage from your own writing about 300 words long. Read the passage once through to remind yourself of the content and main idea. Then do the following:

- Identify two or three places in the passage where the clarity of your writing can be improved. Look for the following:
  - An excessively long sentence that would benefit from being split up into two or three.
  - A few choppy ideas or fragments that would create a better flowing and more logical sentence if they are combined.
- Make revisions as necessary.
- Share your results with a partner. Explain your rationale for making the revisions to them. Seek feedback on your revisions and provide feedback to your partner.

NOTE

1 All examples are retrieved from the Corpus of Contemporary American English (COCA) and come from the following sources: businessinsider.com; jpost.com; Orange County Register; http://bizenglish.adaderana.lk/84318 -2/; entrepreneur.com; and eweek.com. Some sentences were slightly modified for the purposes of the exercise.

🎬 3

Verbs

The Center of the Action

Every sentence must have at least one verb. As the very wise author of *Schoolhouse Rock*, Bob Dorough, said in his famous grammar song, "Verb – that's what's happening." Verbs are words that tell us what somebody is doing, what events are taking place, and what kinds of states things are in. In fact, in English, our whole sentences are constructed around verbs in the same way as tall buildings are constructed around steel frames: verbs provide support and foundation to everything we say or write. We use verbs to do all these things and more:

- Frame topics and arguments
- Make generalizations and conclusions
- Describe processes
- Relate specific events
- Give examples
- Report what somebody else thought, said, or wrote
- Convince the reader of the point we are trying to make
- Express our own stance towards an idea, event, or phenomenon

And to do those things well, so that our readers understand exactly what we are trying to say, we need to choose specific forms of verbs, each with its own job and its own shade of meaning. Verb forms vary quite a lot in English. Verbs can consist of one word, like this:

DOI: 10.4324/9781003159889-4

Our galaxy __contains__ billions of individual stars, clouds of gas, and cosmic dust.

Or they can contain several words, like this:

This situation __could have been avoided__ if we __had asked__ for help right away.

Verb forms can indicate whether the action we are talking about is in the past, present, or future; whether it is actual or hypothetical; and whether it is ongoing or completed at any given point in time.

In this chapter, we will explore how to use verbs appropriately so that we can clearly mark for our readers what it is that we are doing in our texts, be they essays, lab reports, written exam answers, job application letters, workplace memos, or anything else.

This chapter consists of five sections. Each section addresses a particular skill in using verbs for academic and professional writing:

3.1 Recognizing verb forms commonly used in academic and professional writing
3.2 Using verbs to report the ideas and words of others
3.3 Managing verb forms in the flow of text
3.4 Expressing stance through verbs
3.5 Using verbs to emphasize specific aspects of a message

Let's begin.

3.1 WHICH VERB FORMS ARE MOST COMMON?

After you work through this section of the chapter, you will be well on your way to say confidently:

🎯 I can recognize most commonly used verb forms and their meanings.

🎯 I can match the most common verb forms with the kinds of jobs they do in a sentence: relate a story, provide an example, make a generalization, describe a change.

PRACTICE 3.1-A

 Directions: Identifying Usage Patterns

The purpose of this exercise is to draw your attention to how specific verb forms indicate different types of action: continuous, repeated, completed, and so on. The passage below is adapted from a student essay in a composition course.

*   Read the passage carefully.
*   Identify the meaning in context of the verb tense of each bolded verb.
*   Choose the best option from the list below and write your answer next to the corresponding number on the right.

    A.   General facts, regularly repeated actions, or actions currently going on
    B.   Repeated actions in the past
    C.   Completed actions in the past
    D.   Actions beginning in the past and continuing to now
    E.   Others' written ideas or current opinions
    F.   Possible actions or actions that may happen in the future

THE LAZY GENERATION?

Generation Z is stigmatized by the several generations of adults that parent, teach, and interact with them, and the prejudice is unfairly applied to the intellectually motivated students of Gen Z. Gen Z high-school students who are academically driven to succeed are often misunderstood as students who are more likely to slack off and quit when times get tough.

Gen Z students **(1) are** very academically **driven** to succeed because of their parents. Gen X (born as early as the 1960s and as late as the 1980s) **(2) have** firmly **established** that it's "a very tough world out there," and there **(3) is** no such thing as everyone being a winner with no losers (Stillman). These parents **(4) have drilled** this concept into the skulls of their children so much that it **(5) results** in my generation being much more competitive than previous generations. From these repeated ideas, the high schoolers of today **(6) are pushing** themselves to take "too many AP classes in high school rather than too few" (Moody). On average a student focused on STEM in my graduating class **(7) takes** 6 to 7 advanced placement (AP) classes, and a full schedule **(8) could be filled** with only AP classes. As Gen Z high school students, many of my peers and I **(9) take** it upon ourselves to take these rigorous courses in order to have a better life than our parents. We **(10) grew up** knowing that parents **(11) could have** a job one day and **(12) lose** it the next day. We grew up with the extensive library of stories that our parents **(13) would recite** to us if they **(14) sensed** that we **(15) were** not **focusing** enough on school. These stories **(16) would range** from the several miles that they **(17) had to walk** to school to the multiple jobs they **(18) worked** in order to keep the roof over our heads, the lights on, piping hot food on the table, water running, and the list **(19) goes** on. Gen Z students **(20) strive** extremely hard for a life that **(21) is** better than their parents', a life that **(22) shows** that all their parents' hard work **(23) didn't go** to waste.

1. A
2.
3.
4.
5.
6.
7.
8.
9.
10.
11.
12.
13.
14.
15.
16.
17.
18.
19.
20.
21.
22.
23.
24.

🏃 SUMMARY: MOST USED ENGLISH VERB FORMS

Verb Forms	Examples	Uses	Grammatical Term
Base verb Base verb + s	• Our galaxy **contains** billions of individual stars, clouds of gas, and cosmic dust. • Engineers **apply** physical and mathematical concepts in their daily work. • Herbert Freeman, in an introduction to his 1980 IEEE compilation of computer graphics papers, **presents** a succinct overview of the first two decades of the development of the CGI discipline.[1]	• Generalizations • Repeated or routine actions • Timeless facts • Process descriptions • Reports of somebody else's ideas or words	Simple present
Base verb + ed or special form did(not) + base verb	• Kurt Cobain **began** to play music at a young age. • Kurt Cobain and Krist Novoselic **formed** Nirvana in 1987. • Childhood diseases were much more dangerous at the time when vaccines **did not exist**. • If each student **logged** in with their own unique ID, the teacher would see their individual progress.	• Events that took place at a specific time in the past • Facts or phenomena that are no longer true or no longer exist • Reports of somebody else's ideas or words • Imagined or hypothetical conditions	Simple past
Will + base verb	• These charts **will explain** how submarines work. • Without artificial irrigation, almonds **will not grow** in this region.	• Promises • Predictions	Simple future

(Continued)

Verb Forms	Examples	Uses	Grammatical Term
Have + verb + ed/en Has + verb + ed/en	• This 3-D model **has become** a standard of reference in computer graphics. • The results of this research **have found** wide applications in agriculture.	• New developments from the past to the present • Changes from the past to the present • Something that happened in the past but is relevant now	Present perfect
Am/is/are + verb + -ing	• There is no clear evidence that Iran **is developing** nuclear weapons. • We **are working** on plans to provide customers with two additional plans by this fall. • I **am** currently **exploring** all options.	• Events that are currently developing and are not yet complete • Actions or events viewed as temporary	Present progressive
was/were + verb + -ing	• The spokesperson did not comment on whether the agency **was investigating** the attacks. • Many audience members **were recording** the performance on their mobile phones despite the management's request not to do so at the beginning of the show. • I **was wondering** if I could ask you a question.	• Actions or events that were developing at a particular time in the past • Something that was developing but was not finished in the past • Marking the desire not to impose on somebody; politeness	Past progressive

(Continued)

Verb Forms	Examples	Uses	Grammatical Term
can/could/ may/might/ must + base verb	• There is no indication of increased levels of solar activity that **can explain** the current global warming. • Spicy foods **might cause** excessive heartburn in patients with this condition. • Everyone **must follow** the rule of law. • We grew up with the extensive library of stories that our parents **would recite** to us if they sensed that we were not focusing enough on school.	• Making one's claim stronger or weaker, depending on the choice of the word preceding the base verb. See Section 3.4 for more details. • *Would* for repeated actions in the past	Modals

PRACTICE 3.1-B

 ### Directions to Part I: Making Context-Driven Verb Choices

In this exercise, you will practice using appropriate verb forms for making generalizations. The passage below is also an excerpt from "The LaZy Generation" essay used in Practice 3.1-A.

• For each bolded verb, write in the verb form you consider the most appropriate, including the helping verbs where necessary (like *be, am, is, are, was, were, have, has, do, does, did, can, could, may, must, might*).
• Choose forms to **make generalizations** about the topic.
• Remember: in some cases, more than one choice is possible to express slightly different shades of meaning.
• Discuss any differences in choices with a partner after you complete the assignment on your own.

High school Gen Z students actively **(1 focus)** themselves in school because of the stress that they associate with college. As they **(2 progress)** in their journey through high school, students **(3 realize)** that college is closer than they **(4 think)** and that if there is ever a time to work hard it **(5 be)** now. Their performance in these courses **(6 determine)** which colleges will accept them and from there, depending on what path they **(7 choose)** (e.g., medicine, engineering, law), they **(8 start)** to stress about how well they will perform to get into a specialized school. Because high-school students **(9 keep)** in mind that money **(10 not grow)** on trees, they **(11 gravitate)** towards jobs that **(12 offer)** more security. Although few of them are formally in a college class (which can change due to opportunities like Dual Enrollment), they often **(13 hear)** snippets of the worst parts of it, like failing courses because of professors' whims rather than students' performance, being sleep deprived, and lacking time for a personal life. Academically driven students **(14 discuss)** the various shadowing opportunities that they can take and the chances that each one of them **(15 has)** in being accepted to a specific college, factoring in race, financial income, sports, GPA, SAT/ACT scores, etc. High-school students still in their junior year **(16 talk)** about college so much so that they begin to believe that they are as knowledgeable about the process and requirements as the college and university's accepting offices.	1. *focus* 2. 3. 4. 5. 6. 7. 8. 9. 10. 11. 12. 13. 14. 15. 16.

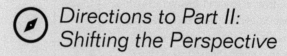

Directions to Part II:
Shifting the Perspective

The goal of this exercise is to help you notice how verb forms change when the writer changes the purpose and genre of their writing from generalization to an account of past events.

- Go back to the passage in Part I and choose verb forms for it again, but this time write **as a young or older adult (your choice) describing what happened to them when they were a Gen-Z teenager.**

For example, number 1 would change from *focus* to *focused* or *have focused*.

PRACTICE 3.1-C

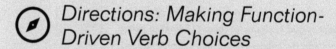

Directions: Making Function-Driven Verb Choices

In this exercise, you will practice making the appropriate choices for verb forms depending on the job each verb does.

- For the passage below, make **consistent** verb form choices.
- Make a choice between making generalizations about the present or discussing actions that have already happened.
- Please note that your choices of verb forms may differ depending on the perspective you take – that of a current young Gen Z individual or an older adult. The choice of the perspective is yours to make. But once you've made it, maintain this perspective so that your verb forms are, indeed, consistent.

Your choice of meaning for this paragraph:
_____ Generalizing
_____ Discussing what has already happened

The immense pressure from parents and the stress that they associate with college **(1 drive)** Generation Z students. Gen Z high school students always **(2 find)** new ways to go around the troubling educational system. These ways **(3 include)** Dual Enrollment or concurrent enrollment classes (which allow high school students to take college classes for college credit), which **(4 be)** incorporated into a student's life afterschool if he/she **(5 choose)** to add it. Gen Z students **(6 sidestep)** this problem by committing to a few colleges and taking the AP classes and tests which **(7 correspond)** to the AP credits that the colleges accept. A beeline for college **(8 be)** the preferred path for Gen Z students, but Gen Z students always **(9 look)** for the easiest path to reach a goal. The result of this **(10 be)** that Gen Z students **(11 appear)** lazy in the eyes of past generations since they **(12 not struggle)** as hard as others to get to their goals, whether that be college, a full-time job, or a life without financial struggle.	1. (*drives, has driven, drove*) 2. 3. 4. 5. 6. 7. 8. 9. 10. 11. 12.

PRACTICE 3.1-D

 Directions: Editing

In this exercise, you will hone your editing skills, focusing on choosing the most suitable verb forms for conveying the author's meaning.

- Read the passage below adapted from a student essay. Some verb forms in this draft are used inappropriately because they don't match the purpose of the writer or the timeline the writer is discussing.
- Read the passage carefully and change the verb forms **where necessary**, identifying the sentence with the number in parentheses.
- Remember: Not every sentence will have an error.
- Provide explanations for the changes you make.

The first paragraph is done as an example. In the second paragraph, the problematic verbs are identified to help you focus your attention. Starting from the third paragraph, you will need to find the problematic verbs yourself.

- Sometimes, more than one choice is possible depending on the meaning the writer wishes to emphasize.

(1) Engineering ethics is the study of moral values engineers need to rely on in their practice. (2) Engineers have to solve many different problems that come up in their work every day. (3) Even though they might be able to solve the main problem, sometimes it **led** them into other issues that **were** related to that problem but **were** not noticed at first. (4) Engineers must observe and analyze every problem thoroughly before they begin looking for solutions.

(5) An engineer has the responsibility to inform the project manager about any negative effect to the public that **will result** from the project. (6) If an engineer **misled** the manager or **gave** false information about the project to the public, it can result in a tragic event. (7) In addition, the engineer can get in trouble for not disclosing problems of any equipment or product that they **discovered**.

(8) For example, in 1928 the St. Francis Dam collapsed and had caused more than $20,000,000 damage. (9) The dam was built two years before in 1926 by William Mulholland who was Chief Engineer for Los Angeles Department of Water and Supply. (10) From the very beginning, there were cracks in the concrete of the dam. (11) It started leaking, but Mulholland kept saying that the cracks are natural and due to concrete curing. He denied that there is a problem. (12) On March 12, 1928, the dam collapsed and flood everything from San Francisco Canyon to Ventura, killing more than 400 people. (13) People blamed Mulholland for the disaster. (14) Even though he was not charged with a crime, Mulholland was disgraced and had to quit his job.

Sentence (3):

led → leads

were related → are related

were not noticed → are not noticed

Explanation: These sentences describe repeated routine actions and generalizations. They should have "base" or "base + s" verbs.

3.2 WHICH VERB FORMS SHOULD I USE FOR REPORTING THE WORK AND IDEAS OF OTHERS?

In academic and professional writing, we often have to use the words, ideas, or the products of work of other people in order to provide a foundation or support for our own arguments. To preserve our credibility and integrity as writers, we must distinguish clearly between what others have said and done before us and our own contributions to the conversation. To do so, we use reporting phrases that signal to the reader when we begin talking about somebody else's work. These phrases often, although not always, call for the use of reporting verbs. The purpose of this section is to familiarize you with the types of reporting verbs and the patterns of their use.

After you work through this section of the chapter, you will be well on your way to say confidently:

🎯 I can identify the specific verbs and verb forms commonly used to report the work, words, and ideas of others.

🎯 I have expanded my own stock of specific verbs and verb forms to report the work, words, and ideas of others.

🎯 I can make the choices of specific verbs and verb forms that most accurately reflect my stance towards the words, work, and ideas of others that I am reporting.

PRACTICE 3.2-A

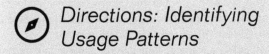 Directions: Identifying Usage Patterns

The purpose of this exercise is for you to identify the structures, including verb forms, that are used to report the **words, ideas, and work products of others**.

Below, you will find three passages in different genres, ranging from research papers, university webpages, to journalistic pieces. All passages contain references to the words, ideas, or work products, such as research results or discoveries, of others that inform and support the points that the author of each passage is trying to make.

Your task for each passage is to:

• Identify the stretches of language that indicate that the author is using somebody else's words or ideas.

• Place these reporting phrases and structures in the table below each passage and identify the form of the verb (if any) used in them. If there is no verb, write down any other indicators that the author is calling on the words, ideas, or work of others.

- Note if each reporting structure presents exact words of the original source, the paraphrasing of the words, a bigger concept or idea from the original, or the product of the source's work. The first example in each passage is done as an example.

- After you examine all the passages and complete the tables after each, discuss the questions below the texts with a partner.

Passage 1

From: Dong, H. B., & Koo, J. (2018). Conspicuous and inconspicuous luxury consumption: A content analysis of BMW advertisements. *Reinvention: An International Journal of Undergraduate Research*, *11*(2). www.warwick.ac.uk/reinventionjournal/archive/volume11issue2/dong.

Conspicuous consumption has long been studied in the field of consumer behavior, dating back to *The Theory of the Leisure Class: An Economic Study of Institutions*, by Thorstein Veblen (1899), in which **Veblen defined** conspicuous consumption as how consumers use material objects to indicate social position, wealth and status. In 1999, Vigeneron and Johnson developed a conceptual framework of prestige-seeking consumer behavior to examine the characteristics of luxury brands. The study found that consumption of luxury goods can bring in interpersonal effects (conspicuous, unique and social) and personal effects (emotional and quality). Each of the five values (conspicuous, unique, social, emotional and quality) is combined with a relevant motivation, categorized as Veblenian, Snob, Bandwagon, Hedonist and Perfectionist (Vigeneron and Johnson, 1999: 3–4).

Besides the work of Vigneron and Johnson, there are other studies that provide different perspectives on why consumers buy luxury goods (Table 1). In the book *Spent: Sex, Evolution, and Consumer Behavior*, Geoffrey F. Miller (2010) applies evolutionary psychological theory to examine how American consumers use conspicuous consumption of luxury goods not only to signal status and wealth but also to communicate biological values, impress potential mates and deter rivals. Using evolutionary psychology, studies carried out by Saad and Vongas (2009) and Hennighausen *et al.* (2016) examined the use of conspicuous consumption of luxury goods to display self-confidence, dominance and attractiveness. On the other hand, Berger and Ward (2010) and Wilson, Eckhardt and Belk (2015) discussed the inconspicuous consumption of luxury goods with low brand prominence as a way for wealthy consumers with low need for status to signal within-group identity and non-conformity and experience personal satisfaction.

Reporting Structure or Phrase	Verb Form	What Follows the Verb: Somebody's Words, Somebody's Ideas, or Somebody's Work Product
Verblen defined	Defined – base+ed (past tense)	idea

Passage 2

From: Sapers, J. (2011, December 15). *Fighting stereotype threat in the workplace. TC Today.* www.tc.columbia.edu/articles/2011/december/fighting-stereotype-threat-in-the-workplace/.

Stereotype threat, a concept pioneered by social scientist Claude Steele, is the extent to which the perception of being stereotyped influences a person's performance. For example, **researchers have shown that** women may do worse on a math test than male counterparts if they're told, as they sit down to take the test, that women have fared more poorly on the test in the past—or, more broadly, that women simply aren't good at math. Similarly, when white adults are told, just prior to taking a test of unconscious racial attitudes, that whites typically react more positively to white faces than faces of color, they will generally reveal more negative racial attitudes on the test.

Based on these and other findings, Roberson and Kulik argue the need for safeguards in many common workplace situations. Take, for example, a white manager who goes out of her way to give an employee of color a so-called stretch assignment that might represent an opportunity for advancement. Since stereotype threat occurs on the most difficult tasks, the manager needs to be aware of that risk and to help the employee develop strategies for screening out or coping with undermining signals from others. "Managers who aren't aware of stereotype threat and give stretch assignments might see failure, because coping with stereotype threat takes up cognitive resources," Roberson says. "And when employees are struggling with it, they don't have enough resources to work on the task at hand."

Reporting Structure or Phrase	Verb Form	What Follows the Verb: Somebody's Words, Somebody's Ideas, or Somebody's Work Product
Researchers have shown that	Have shown – have + verb + en (present perfect)	Work product – research results

Passage 3

From: Cabrera, A. (2020, 3 June). "Ring down the curtain": What protests mean for a nation already in crisis. *Grist.* https://grist.org/justice/what-protests-mean-for-a-nation-already-in-crisis-george-floyd-rodney-king/.

This inequity is something that **the writer and activist James Baldwin so eloquently addressed in _The Fire Next Time_,** which he published at a critical moment for the civil rights movement in 1963. He argued that there is no possibility of real change in the status of African Americans without the most radical and far-reaching changes in the country's political and social structure. Baldwin originally wrote part of the book as an essay for his nephew to mark the 100th anniversary of the emancipation of enslaved Americans. Despite the Emancipation Proclamation, Baldwin argued, American society was rebuilt on a separate and unequal foundation. Progressive steps toward racial equality were often gestures of tokenism. They never fixed the flaws, the "hard problems," within our systems, so gaping disparities in areas like education and criminal justice persisted. By refusing to examine and confront those hard problems, the American dream had become a "nightmare," wrote Baldwin. He warned of a reckoning: "The Negroes of this country may never be able to rise to power, but they are very well placed indeed to precipitate chaos and ring down the curtain on the American dream."

Reporting Structure or Phrase	Verb Form	What Follows the Verb: Somebody's Words, Somebody's Ideas, or Somebody's Work Product
the writer and activist James Baldwin so eloquently addressed in *The Fire Next Time*	Addressed – base+ed (past tense)	Idea, concept

PRACTICE 3.2-B

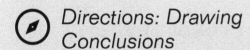

Directions: Drawing Conclusions

In this exercise, you will continue to increase your awareness of the patterns which reporting verbs follow.

- Discuss the following questions with a partner.
- Remember: your goal is to examine how other writers use reporting phrases and to make observations about possible regularities or patterns in such use. There is no one definitive answer to the questions below.
- Try and come to a common view on these questions, but do not expect to find the one and only one correct answer.

Question	Answer
Which three verb forms occur in reporting the words of others most commonly? Provide examples from the texts above to support your point of view.	
Which verbs tend to introduce the words of the source? Which verbs tend to introduce ideas? Which verbs tend to introduce work products, such as discoveries or research results? Provide examples from the texts above to support your point of view.	
Are there any patterns in the use of past, present, or present perfect tense? What do you think drives the author's choice of one verb form over another? Provide examples from the texts above to support your point of view.	

SUMMARY: VERB FORMS USED FOR REPORTING

- The most common verb forms for reporting the words, ideas, and work products of others are:
  - Base verb (argue) or base + s (endorses): (*simple present*)
  - Base + ed (examined) or special form (found): (*simple past*)
  - Have/has + base-ed/en (have shown): (*present perfect*)
- There is no one rigid rule as to which of these forms must be used when. Rather, there are **flexible** tendencies in verb form choice.
  - Writers may choose among all three forms to suit their purposes.
  - Verb form **consistency** within a paragraph is often the most important factor in choosing the form of a reporting verb.

Base verb or base + s (*simple present*)

Meaning/Usage	Examples
Most frequently used to report information that is viewed by the author as the general truth or information most relevant to the author's own argument	Based on these and other findings, Roberson and Kulik **argue** the need for safeguards in many common workplace situations. While Alma Harris broadly **endorses** distributed leadership, Helen Gunter **is more skeptical**, arguing that it is a way of encouraging teachers to do more work, a form of disguised managerialism (Fitzgerald and Gunter, 2006).
Most frequently used with verbs of speaking, thinking, and writing rather than specific accomplishments	"Managers who aren't aware of stereotype threat and give stretch assignments might see failure, because coping with stereotype threat takes up cognitive resources," Roberson **says**. A recent study from Northwestern University **corroborates** Agostini's experience, suggesting that the stress of racial discrimination may partly explain the persistent gaps in academic performance between some nonwhite students, mainly black and Latino youth, and their white counterparts.

Base verb + ed or special form (*simple past*)

Meaning/Usage	Examples
Tends to indicate that the author considers the reported information somewhat outdated, contradictory, or less relevant to the author's own argument Past tense may also be used when a specific date of the source is given, but it is not mandatory	Using evolutionary psychology, studies carried out by Saad and Vongas (2009) and Hennighausen *et al.* (2016) **examined** the use of conspicuous consumption of luxury goods to display self-confidence, dominance and attractiveness. *On the other hand,* Berger and Ward (2010) and Wilson, Eckhardt and Belk (2015) **discussed** the inconspicuous consumption of luxury goods with low brand prominence as a way for wealthy consumers with low need for status to signal within-group identity and non-conformity and experience personal satisfaction.
Tends to be used with verbs referring to specific accomplishments rather than verbs of speaking and writing	The team of researchers **found** that the physiological response to race-based stressors—be it perceived racial prejudice, or the drive to outperform negative stereotypes—leads the body to pump out more stress hormones in adolescents from traditionally marginalized groups. In 1999, Vigeneron and Johnson **developed** a conceptual framework of prestige-seeking consumer behavior to examine the characteristics of luxury brands.

Have/has + base verb with -en or -ed (*present perfect*)

Meaning/Usage	Examples
Most frequently used to indicate that a particular accomplishment or idea is a new development or is particularly close to the writer's own argument	For example, **researchers have shown that** women may do worse on a math test than male counterparts if they're told, as they sit down to take the test, that women have fared more poorly on the test in the past—or, more broadly, that women simply aren't good at math.

SUMMARY: SPECIFIC VERBS AND PATTERNS

Rather than relying on vague reporting verbs, like *says*, *states*, and *writes* over and over, academic and professional writers use more specific verbs. These specific terms either have connotations to show the author's emotions and/or their attitude toward the source, or are more neutral in tone, but show how the author is presenting the information.

There are common patterns in language, so the chart below includes words that are commonly used with the verbs: *of*, *to*, *on*, *that*, nouns, or words with -ing endings (e.g., *researching, eliminating, purchasing*).

Verbs that show the author's emotion and/ or your attitude toward the source	Verbs that show how the author is presenting the information (what the author is doing)	
accuse _____ *of*	add *that* or *to*	invite _____ *to*
admit *to* or *that*	advise *that*	learn *that*
argue *that*	agree *that*	maintain *that*
believe *that*	analyze *noun* or *-ing*	observe *that*
boast *that*	announce *that*	point out *that*
challenge _____ *to*	comment *that* or *on*	propose *that*
claim *that*	compare _____ *to*	question *noun* or *-ing*
criticize _____ *for*	contend *that*	realize *that*
consider *noun* or *-ing*	corroborate	reason *that*
deny *noun, -ing,* or *that*	demonstrate *that*	recommend *that*
dismiss *noun* or *-ing*	describe *noun* or *-ing*	remark *on*
feel *that*	discover *that*	reply *that*
hope *that*	discuss *noun* or *-ing*	report *on* or *that*
imagine *that*	emphasize *that*	request *that*
insist *that*	encourage *noun, -ing,* or _____ *to*	respond *that*
praise _____ *for*	estimate *that*	reveal *that*
prefer *noun, -ing,* or *to*	evaluate *noun* or *-ing*	review *noun* or *-ing*
refuse *to*	examine *noun* or *-ing*	show *that*
subscribe *to*	explain *that*	suggest *that* or *-ing*
threaten *that*	explore *noun* or *-ing*	stress *that*
warn _____ *of/about*	find *that*	understand *that*
	indicate *that*	
	instruct *that* or _____ *to*	

PRACTICE 3.2-C

Directions: Identifying Meaning

The purpose of this exercise is for you to notice the meaning and the attitude the writer shows with the reporting verb choices. Pay attention to bolded verbs and discuss the questions below with a partner or small group.

In his *Forbes* article, "The Debate about GMO Safety is Over, Thanks to a New Trillion-Meal Study," John Entine (1) **accuses** anti-GMO (genetically modified organisms) websites **of** hysterically making claims about the dangers of GMOs on animals and humans without credible sources.

Entine (2) **insists that** anti-GMO "crusaders" rely on anecdotal evidence, non-peer-reviewed journals, and self-published research and (3) **doubts that** farmers would miss the cancerous tumors that should appear in their GMO-fed livestock.

He (4) **boasts that** we can rely instead on "the most comprehensive study of GMOs and food ever conducted" which was published in the *Journal of Animal Science* in 2014.

In their research, University of California-Davis Department of Animal Science geneticist Alison Van Eenennaam and research assistant Amy E. Young (4) **evaluated** "29 years of livestock productivity and health data" of more than 100 billion animals from when animal feed was 100% non-GMO to when it jumped to 90% or more genetically modified (GM) feed.

Van Eenennaam and Young (5) **revealed** that there are no unusual trends in the health of animals since the introduction of GM feed and that their large dataset (6) **indicated** that GM feed is nutritionally equivalent to non-GM feed.

Question	Answer
What does each verb reveal about the writer's attitude toward the source or the emotions of the source's author?	
What does each verb show about the what the source's author does in the source, or how the source's author presents the information?	
How do the specific verbs affect the readers, their view of the writer, and their view of the sources differently than if the writer used *says* and *states* throughout the passage?	
Why does the author use different verb forms (verb + s and verb + ed) for the different sources?	

PRACTICE 3.2-D

 Directions: Editing

In this exercise, you will hone your editing skills, focusing on choosing the most suitable verb forms for conveying the author's meaning.

* Read the passage below, which is an excerpt from an analysis of another author's argument. Some verb forms in this draft are inconsistent or vague.
* Read the passage carefully and change the verb forms where necessary, identifying the sentence with the number in parentheses.
* Keep in mind: not every sentence will have an error.
* Remember that sometimes, more than one choice is possible depending on the meaning the writer wishes to emphasize.

Many heated debates in the United States are based on moral issues. Citizens on both sides of the political spectrum are concerned with the value of life and who makes decisions about our bodies. The arguments are even more complex when both of these issues are involved. Although hundreds of thousands of Americans are in need of organs each year, the US does not have enough donors to meet the need and does not legally allow citizens to put a price on human body parts, like organs. Joanna MacKay, in her essay "Organ Sales Will Saves Lives," says that the US should legalize the sale of human organs, particularly the sale of kidneys to cure renal failure. MacKay shows uninformed voters why they should change their view of organ sales and actively support its legalization.

MacKay used sympathy and logic to gain the support of voters when she informs them about prospective organ sellers. She states that legal organ sales would be beneficial for the possible sellers in poverty in other countries, who are already willing to do so. By describing how the potential sellers "barely have anything to eat, living in shacks and sleeping on dirt floors," she encouraged her readers to feel pity for them. Then she gives a picture of a better life after a kidney sale because they are able to improve their quality of life with the money. The contrasting before and after situations makes those uninformed about the issue see the perspective of potential sellers, who may not have other ways to support themselves or their families. The problem-solution connection of the ideas allows the audience to see that the sale of nonessential organs is a logical option for those in poverty to better their lives and become self-sufficient. Voting to support legalization of organ sales seems to be empowering to those in poverty, and therefore, appealing to voters sympathetic to the disadvantaged and to voters who value entrepreneurism. Although some may worry that the living conditions described would make the organs less healthy, McKay explains that the legalization of organ sales would include evaluating the organs according to strict medical qualifications whereas the black market doesn't.

PRACTICE 3.2-E

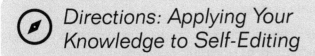 **Directions: Applying Your Knowledge to Self-Editing**

The ultimate goal of all of these practices is to improve your writing, so this practice asks you to apply what you have learned to your essays and reports. Choose one writing assignment that you are currently working on. This can be an assignment for any class. If you have no assignment in progress, choose a paper you wrote for any class before. Edit your draft to use specific verbs to report the words or ideas from others and to use consistent, appropriate verb forms.

3.3 HOW DO I MANAGE VERB FORMS IN THE FLOW OF THE TEXT?

Drawing conclusions and making general claims based on specific evidence is part and parcel of writing both in the classroom and in the workplace. As proficient readers, we rely on subtle cues in the writer's choice of grammatical structures and words to understand when this writer is making a generalization – i.e., a statement about things that are true in many situations – and when she is giving concrete examples that have led her to this generalization. One of the tools writers draw on to help their readers distinguish between examples and generalizations is the choice of verb forms. In this section, you will examine and practice such choices in order to be able to make the distinctions between examples and general claims clear to your own readers.

After you work through this section of the chapter, you will be well on your way to say confidently:

⊚ I can distinguish between specific evidence and general claims in a text I am reading.

⊚ I can made deliberate choices of verb forms in my own writing to signal generalizations or specific examples.

⊚ I can identify and use phrases signaling the shift from examples to generalizations and vice versa.

PRACTICE 3.3-A

 Directions: Identifying Usage Patterns

This exercise is designed to help you identify how verb forms are used to signal the writer's general claims about groups, events, or actions and specific evidence that supports such claims. The text below is an excerpt of a short article on linguistic profiling from *Psychology Today*.

• First, read the text and identify each marked passage as conveying either a general claim or a specific example or event. A box for doing so has been provided next to each passage.
  A: Statement of a general claim, fact, or truth
  B: Specific example, event, or action
• Second, examine the bold-faced verb forms and determine which of them tend to signal generalizations, and which ones tend to signal specific examples or events.

- Third, write out the patterns of using verb forms for general claims and specific examples in the space provided below. Use your own words to formulate these patterns.

The first passage has been marked up as an example.

From: Fridland, V. (2020, June 11). The sound of racial profiling: When language leads to discrimination. *Psychology Today: Language in the Wild Blog.* www.psychologytoday.com/us/blog/language-in -the-wild/202006/the-sound-racial-profiling.

The Sound of Racial Profiling: When language leads to discrimination Given the recent protests and riots stemming from the killing of George Floyd, many **have been left** wondering how racism **might be infused** into less obvious facets of our lives. While his death certainly **throws** stark light on the continuing danger of being Black in America, it also **makes** us face the inequities that **pervade** our society. But bias **is not only based** on how we **look**. It'**s often also related** to how we **speak**, and this **raises** the question of how the way we **react** to what people **say** **is influenced** by the color of their skin.	General claims. Statements of general facts/truth. Verb forms: • Base (simple <u>present</u>) • Have + verb+ed (<u>present</u> perfect) • Modal + verb
As a sociolinguist who specializes in how social identity and language **are connected**, this is a question that has very much been on my mind lately. The credibility, employability, or criminality we **assign** to voices **can have** a very real impact on those who **happen to speak** (or even just **look** like they **speak**) non-standard dialects. **Linguistic hallucinations?** If you happen to be one of the roughly 25% of Americans who identifies as an ethnic minority, there is a good chance that you have been the victim of linguistic bias, even if you speak standard English. Linguistic research on the impact of stereotypes **shows** we **can hallucinate** an accent just by seeing an ethnic looking face.	

(Continued)

A number of studies **have looked** at how simply telling someone they **are listening** to an ethnic speaker or showing them a photo of an ethnic face (while playing a standard speech recording) **influences** the perception of accentedness or non-standardness and **lowers** scores on intelligibility and competence scales. This, further research **suggests**, **can influence** the scores non-native instructors **receive** on teaching evaluations and **lower** the expectations teachers **have** for the educational achievement of African-American children.

What exactly do we mean by linguistic profiling?

More broadly, research both in linguistics and social psychology **has looked** at how subtle and often unconscious linguistic practices **predispose** us to react to and think about people differently depending on their race.

Current Washington University and former Stanford professor John Baugh **coined** the term 'linguistic profiling' several years ago in response to the discrimination he himself **experienced** when looking for a house in majority-White Palo Alto.

In a study he **designed** with colleagues, Baugh, using either African-American, Chicano or Standard accented English (called linguistic guises), **made** calls inquiring about property for rent. When using non-standard accents, the property listed **was** somehow no longer available, in contrast to when he **was using** his standard English guise. His work **was** the basis for a widely seen public service campaign to advocate for fair housing practices.

But what exactly **are we tuning** into when we **'hear'** ethnicity in voices? We **might think** people **sound** Black or Latino, but, since we clearly sometimes **imagine** accents where there **isn't** one, **are** we even very good at recognizing race on the basis of speech alone? In short, yes.

When we **hear** certain linguistic clues, things like pronouncing 'th' sounds as a 'v' or deleting 'r' sounds (i.e., "brovah" for brother) or third-person singular deletion ("he go"), we **do often identify** those features as part of ethnic varieties. But, even less salient aspects of our speech **seem to signal** ethnic identity and, potentially, **trigger** activation of stereotyped associations.

(Continued)

In a follow-up to the study described above, linguists Purnell, Idsardi and Baugh **found** that listeners **were able to determine** speakers' ethnicity as quickly as the first word said in the phone conversation at around 70% accuracy. In other words, listeners **had** them at "hello." The researchers **discovered**, even without the use of widely recognizable linguistic features like those just mentioned, listeners **were sensitive** to very subtle phonetic cues such as how the 'e' vowel in "hello" **was pronounced**.	
Of course, recognizing that some language features **might indicate** someone's gender, age or race itself **is not** problematic, and, in fact, something we all **do**. But associating them with generalized negative traits or discriminating against them on the basis of these presumed traits **is** where the inherent danger **lies**. Often these negative associations **are not overt**, and we **might not even be aware** of doing it, but instead **are implicit** in how we **make** decisions about how we **are going to interact with or evaluate** those we **hear**.	

Patterns:

General claims, conclusions, general truth:

_____

_____

_____

_____

_____

_____

Specific examples, events, and evidence:

_____

_____

_____

_____

_____

_____

PRACTICE 3.3-B

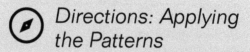

Directions: Applying the Patterns

In this task, you will practice applying the patterns you have deduced in Practice 3.3-A. The text below is the second half of the same article on linguistic profiling. Certain verbs in it have been placed in their base form in parentheses.

- Choose the appropriate verb form to fit the context of each sentence, paragraph, and the text overall. Focus on the meaning – is the author making a generalization or is she talking about a specific example?
- Provide an explanation for your choices.
- Keep in mind – sometimes more than one form is possible, and the choice of the past vs. present may be driven by the verb form consistency in the whole paragraph.

From: Fridland, V. (2020, June 11). The sound of racial profiling: When language leads to discrimination. *Psychology Today: Language in the Wild Blog.* www.psychologytoday.com/us/blog/language-in -the-wild/202006/the-sound-racial-profiling.

Text	Verb form choice and explanation
Such consequences are magnified in the criminal justice system	
Research by linguists John Rickford and Sharese King illustrated how linguistic bias might have affected the outcome in the trial of George Zimmerman for the shooting of Trayvon Martin in 2012. Zimmerman, who (**1 claim**) the shooting (**2 be**) in self-defense, (**3 be found**) not guilty of second-degree murder. A potential contributor to this outcome was the prosecution's key witness Rachel Jeantel's use of African-American English. She (**4 be ridiculed**) as inarticulate, not credible and incomprehensible, and, due to unfamiliarity with the dialect, court transcripts of her testimony (**5 be**) highly inaccurate.	1. 2. 3. 4. 5.
As Rickford and King's work highlights, the lack of credibility and unintelligibility associated with disfavored linguistic varieties could affect judicial rulings. Driving that point home, subsequent research on juror appraisals (**6 find**) an increase in negative evaluations and guilty verdicts when witnesses (**7 speak**) African-American English.	6. 7.
This problem, of course, (**8 be**) not limited to contexts where African-American English varieties (**9 be involved**), as non-native speakers are also unfairly disadvantaged in court and other institutional settings as a result of linguistic barriers. And even for those who never (**10 see**) the inside of a courtroom, speaking a disfavored variety has been shown to lead to increased discrimination in housing practices, in the educational system and in hiring contexts.	8. 9. 10.
Some might suggest this is simply a reason for speakers to adopt standard dialects, but, as discussed above, just looking like you might speak something other than Standard English can predispose listeners to hear an accent even if it (**11 not exist**). So, the problem is not really with the speech itself, but with the attitudes we (**12 hold**) about the speakers of these dialects.	11. 12.
The real solution is, of course, to work to reduce and, eventually, eradicate linguistic prejudice by taking the time to understand the socio-historical and linguistic underpinnings of non-standard varieties. After all, recalling the keen observation of linguist Max Weinreich, "A language is a dialect with an army and a navy." Thus, for a non-standard dialect speaker, the fight is far from fair.	

REFERENCES

Kurinec, Courtney, & Charles Weaver III. (2019). Dialect on trial: Use of African American Vernacular English influences juror appraisals. *Psychology, Crime & Law, 25*(8), 803–828.

Purnell, T., Idsardi, W., & Baugh, J. (1999). Perceptual and phonetic experiments on American English dialect identification. *Journal of Language and Social Psychology, 18*, 10–31.

Rickford, John R., & King, Sharese. (2016). Language and linguistics on trial: Hearing Rachel Jeantel (and other vernacular speakers) in the courtroom and beyond. *Language, 92*(4), 948–988.

PRACTICE 3.3-C

 Directions: Identifying Usage Patterns

The purpose of this exercise is to focus your attention on the signals that writers use to prepare the reader for the shift in the type of information they present in their work and the accompanying shift in the verb forms. The passage you will be reading is an excerpt from an introductory college psychology textbook.

- Read the passage and underline or highlight all verbs.
- Note places where the continuous use of present verb forms (base, base+s, have/has + verb+ed, am/is/are + verb+ing) shifts to past verb forms (base+ed or special form or was/were + verb+ing) and vice versa.
- Circle any phrases that indicate the need to use present or past tense forms.
- Answer the questions following the reading to identify the patterns.
- Discuss your answers with a partner.

Excerpt from: Spielman, R. M., Jenkins, W. J., & Lovett, M. D. (2020). *Psychology 2e*. Rice University: Open Stax. Full text is available for free at https://openstax.org/details/psychology-2e.

Multicultural and Cross-Cultural Psychology

Culture has important impacts on individuals and social psychology, yet the effects of culture on psychology are under-studied. [...] Multicultural psychologists develop theories and conduct research with diverse populations, typically within one country. Cross-cultural psychologists compare populations across countries, such as participants from the United States compared to participants from China.

In 1920, Francis Cecil Sumner was the first African American to receive a PhD in psychology in the United States. Sumner established a psychology degree program at Howard University, leading to the education of a new generation of African American psychologists (Black, Spence, and Omari, 2004). Much of the work of early psychologists from diverse backgrounds was dedicated to challenging intelligence testing and promoting innovative educational methods for children. George I. Sanchez contested such testing with Mexican American children. As a psychologist of Mexican heritage, he pointed out that the language and cultural barriers in testing were keeping children from equal opportunities (Guthrie, 1998). By 1940, he was teaching with his doctoral degree at University of Texas at Austin and challenging segregated educational practices (Romo, 1986).

Two famous African American researchers and psychologists are Mamie Phipps Clark and her husband, Kenneth Clark. They are best known for their studies conducted on African American children and doll preference, research that was instrumental in the *Brown v. Board of Education* Supreme Court desegregation case. The Clarks applied their research to social services and opened the first child guidance center in Harlem (American Psychological Association, 2019).

Questions to discuss with a partner:

a. What kinds of phrases can be used to signpost a shift in the verb forms for the reader?

    _____

    _____

    _____

    _____

    _____

    _____

b. Where in the text or sentence can these phrases occur?

    _____

    _____

    _____

    _____

    _____

    _____

c. How can these phrases help the reader follow the text smoothly?

    _____

    _____

    _____

    _____

    _____

    _____

PRACTICE 3.3-D

 ## Directions: Editing

In this exercise, you will be applying the skills and knowledge of verb forms you have gained so far to editing an excerpt from a draft of a student's essay.

- First, read through the passage to get the general idea what the author is trying to say.
- Read the passage the second time, underlining or highlighting all verbs. Mark each verb form as base verb or base+s (present), base+ed or the special past tense form (past), have/has + base+ed/en (present perfect), or am/is/are + base+ing (present progressive).
- Evaluate whether the writer's intended purpose matches his choice of verb forms:
  - Base verb or base+s (present) for generalizations
  - Base+ed (past) for specific examples
  - Am/is/are + verb+ing (present progressive) for ongoing actions or events
  - Have/has + verb+en/ed (present perfect) for new developments and changes that are relevant to now
- Change the verb forms to match the writer's purpose as necessary. Keep in mind that in some cases, both past and present forms are possible depending on the author's purpose. Verb form consistency (present or past) in the timeframe of the paragraph is usually the main factor in making the choice in such situations.
- Read the passage again, noting whether there are appropriate signals for verb form shifts in the places where the framework shifts from past to present and vice versa. Such signals can include, among others:
  - Phrases indicating time (*at 8:00 AM, when I was in high school,* etc.)
  - Frequency phrases (*usually, never, as a rule,* etc.)
  - Phrases introducing examples, opinions, conclusions, and so on (*I believe, in my case,* etc.)
- Insert such signal words where necessary.

School Should Start Later

High school in the U.S. usually starts at about 8:00 AM. It should start later. Why? Simply because students don't get enough sleep. Students who sleep less than eight hours a night have been less alert in their classes. Teenagers feel sleepy throughout their day and fall into "microsleeps," which is also called daydreaming. This makes them lose valuable information the teacher presented in class. When I was in high school, I have been caught in these "micro-sleeps" several times, and I have missed information that was crucial for the exams and my grades. If school starts later in the morning, students won't lose valuable information due to falling asleep in class.

Having obligations besides school also prevents students from getting enough sleep. For example, some students have to work, but the work has a negative effect on the time they can spend on their education. In my case, I work part time and attend school full time. I arrive home exhausted from the long day first at school and then at work and begin my homework late. I can't go to bed until after midnight. This makes it hard to study and it is challenging for my grades. Because high school starts early, I had to get up at 6:00 AM to be at school on time. Now, I have to commute to school, so I have to get up even earlier.

Clubs and sports also interfered with sleep. Students become engaged in extracurricular activities that they are interested in, such as sports and clubs. When I was in high school, I was told that having several extracurricular activities is important when applying to college. That is why I was in two different clubs, and I was on the track team. Having school, work, clubs, family and friends time fills up my agenda leaving me little to no time to sleep. I believe that less should be expected of students so that they have time to be students.

PRACTICE 3.3-E

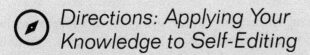 Directions: Applying Your
Knowledge to Self-Editing

Now, it's time to apply your editing skills to your own writing.

- Choose a piece you have previously written for any class. This passage should be between 300 and 500 words long.
- Follow the steps from Practice 3.3-D above to edit your writing for appropriate verb forms, verb tense shifts, and clear signposting of such shifts.
- Reflect on any changes you have made: Which forms and functions seemed to need the most correction? What can you do when you write next time to avoid making unclear choices in verb forms and verb form shift signals? Jot down notes on your reflections below.

_____

_____

_____

_____

_____

_____

_____

_____

_____

_____

3.4 HOW CAN I SHOW MY ATTITUDE AND STANCE THROUGH VERB FORMS?

Although writing in college and the workplace is expected to be largely fact-based and driven by logical reasoning, there is certainly room for writers to express their own attitude to the content of their written pieces. We call this attitude *stance*. Stance is the writer's projection of their own authority, confidence, degree of commitment to, or belief about the topic they are addressing. Writers can position themselves, for example, as somewhat hesitant about tentative results of their research, or as being modest in their claims, or as providing options rather than commands in their recommendations. Similarly, they can take on a stance of strong authority, assertiveness, and confidence with regard to what they are saying.

Neither cautious nor bold positioning is wrong in and of itself. Different types of claims require different stances on the part of the writer. Every writer needs to know how to soften their claims to prevent these claims from sounding too sweeping and indiscriminate or how to boost the claims to ensure that readers take them seriously.

You have already explored how to express your stance towards the words, ideas, and work of others through specific reporting structures, including concrete verbs. In this section, you will learn how to use *modals* to express your stance towards other elements of writing, such as your own generalizations, conclusions, and recommendations.

Modals are nine special words – often labeled as modal verbs – that allow speakers and writers to express their attitudes towards the actions denoted by actual verbs. These words are:

May	Might	Can
Could	Shall	Should
Will	Would	Must

PRACTICE 3.4-A

Directions: Identifying Usage Patterns

This exercise is designed to focus your attention on the functions and meanings of verbs containing modals.

- First, read the two passages below, focusing on the underlined verbs. Decide, for each verb, if it expresses:
  A. A definite prediction
  B. A strong possibility
  C. A tentative possibility
  D. An option
  E. An ability
  F. A suggestion
  G. A strong recommendation
  H. A forceful command

You do not have to find a verb corresponding to each label. Focus on your understanding of the writer's intended meaning as a reader.

- Write the letters corresponding to the functions above (A–H) next to the number of each verb in the right-hand column. There may be more than one interpretation of each modal's meaning.
- Discuss your decisions with a partner or a group. Make a note of any patterns or groupings of modals that you observe.
- Fill out the table below with your answers. More than one correct answer is possible.

Both excerpts are from: Esri (2008, September). *Essays on geography and GIS*. Esri.[2]

Introduction. In ESRI (2008, September), *Essays on geography and GIS*, p. 3. Esri.

What is GIS?	1. B and/ or G
Making decisions based on geography is basic to human thinking. Where (1) **shall we go**, what (2) **will it be** like, and what (3) **shall we do** when we get there are applied to the simple event of going to the store or to the major event of launching a bathysphere into the ocean's depths. By understanding geography and people's relationship to location, we (4) **can make** informed decisions about the way we live on our planet. A geographic information system (GIS) is a technological tool for comprehending geography and making intelligent decisions.	2. A 3. 4.
GIS organizes geographic data so that a person reading a map (5) **can select** data necessary for a specific project or task. A thematic map has a table of contents that allows the reader to add layers of information to a basemap of real-world locations. For example, a social analyst (6) **might use** the basemap of Eugene, Oregon, and select datasets from the U.S. Census Bureau to add data layers to a map that shows residents' education levels, ages, and employment status. With an ability to combine a variety of datasets in an infinite number of ways, GIS is a useful tool for nearly every field of knowledge from archaeology to zoology.	5. 6.
A good GIS program is able to process geographic data from a variety of sources and integrate it into a map project. Many countries have an abundance of geographic data for analysis, and governments often make GIS datasets publicly available. Map file databases often come included with GIS packages; others (7) **can be obtained** from both commercial vendors and government agencies. Some data is gathered in the field by global positioning units that attach a location coordinate (latitude and longitude) to a feature such as a pump station.	7.
GIS maps are interactive. On the computer screen, map users (8) **can scan** a GIS map in any direction, zoom in or out, and change the nature of the information contained in the map. They (9) **can choose** whether to see the roads, how many roads to see, and how roads (10) **should be depicted**. Then they (11) **can select** what other items they wish to view alongside these roads such as storm drains, gas lines, rare plants, or hospitals. Some GIS programs are designed to perform sophisticated calculations for tracking storms or predicting erosion patterns. GIS applications (12) **can be embedded** into common activities such as verifying an address.	8. 9. 10. 11. 12.
From routinely performing work-related tasks to scientifically exploring the complexities of our world, GIS gives people the geographic advantage to become more productive, more aware, and more responsive citizens of planet Earth.	

From: Dobson, J. (2008, September). Bring back geography! In ESRI, *Essays on geography and GIS*, p. 47. Esri.

Bring Back Geography!	
By Jerome Dobson	
Restoring geography is in your best interest as a citizen of the world and especially as a GIS professional, regardless of your home discipline. We are your natural ally, whether you yourself hold a degree in geography or not. No discipline (13) **should rest easy** until the one that was lost is restored. Every scholar (14) **should be clamoring** for geography's return as proof that future purges (15) **will not be tolerated**, and that holds true even for those who do not like geography.	13. 14. 15.
What protects other disciplines from onslaughts like those that beset geography? You (16) **may imagine** that public opposition would be fierce, and legions of academic peers (17) **would rise up** in arms, but that did not happen in our case. You (18) **may imagine** that your own discipline (19) **would not go down** without a fight, but geographers accepted their fate far more graciously than they (20) **should have**. Earlier this year, when I published an op-ed piece questioning how and why the nationwide purge had occurred, all but one of the public replies came from geographers, and several blamed the discipline itself. Yet every reason they offered was characteristic of many other disciplines, none of which were punished as we were.	16. 17. 18. 19. 20.

Meaning	Possible Modals
a. A definite prediction	
b. A strong possibility	
c. A tentative possibility	
d. An option	
e. An ability	
f. A suggestion	
g. A recommendation	
h. A forceful command	

🏃 SUMMARY: MODALS' FUNCTIONS

Modals do two main jobs:

1. Convey to the reader the writer's degree of certainty about the actions or events she is describing
2. Urge the reader to adopt particular behaviors or perform particular actions.

The choice of a modal shows the reader how strongly – or weakly – the writer feels about the actions expressed by the verbs.

Levels of Certainty		
Very certain	Will Must	The trend towards internet connectivity in electronic devices **will** continue to increase over the next decade. There **must** be grants available for student research. We are certain of it.
Fairly certain	Should Can	A new analysis **should** render more reliable findings. When we cough or sneeze, the droplets containing viruses **can** land on surfaces and contaminate them.
Somewhat uncertain	May Could Might	Forensic engineering is most commonly used in civil law cases. However, it **may** also be used in some criminal investigations. The new analytical model **could** help predict the conditions for the existence of life on extrasolar planets. Using a warm blanket **might** be the best choice for battling the chills.

(Continued)

Levels of Obligation		
Strong urging or forceful command	Must Will Shall (very rare; more often used legal documents)	To be well informed, you **must** seek out information from a variety of sources and **must** be able to evaluate the credibility and validity of this information. When directed, all selected applicants **will** report at the HR manager's office. All medical records **shall** be provided to the patient within 24 hours of the written request.
Strong recommendation	Should	Every high school graduate **should** reach college with the knowledge that geography is a possible major with strong career prospects.
Suggestion	Can Could Might (want to) May (want to)	Students working on research papers **can** seek help from their subject librarian. Using this platform, students **could** revise their papers and resubmit them quickly, or they **could** seek feedback from peers before doing so. There is no time like the present to begin investing in your future, so you **might want to** explore the best options for you. Forest Hills residents **may want to** check their fruit trees for psyllid infestations.

Other Means of Boosting and Softening Claims

In addition to specific verbs and modals, claims can be strengthened or softened by the use of particular adjectives, adverbs, nouns, and even phrases. The table below presents some examples, although the list is far from exhaustive.

Softening	Boosting
Adjectives	
Some studies show that children of divorce are less <u>likely</u> to get a college degree. We have identified several **probable** cases of SARS-like illness... <u>**Possible**</u> considerations include the alteration of treatment and supportive care.	These findings are <u>**significant**</u> because... The results are <u>indisputable</u>. Scientists have found **conclusive** evidence of...
Adverbs	
The rates could fall as much as 40%, but the estimate, <u>**admittedly**</u>, contains a significant margin of error. Continuing the course of medication without changes is <u>**potentially**</u> risky. Extreme stress can <u>**sometimes**</u> even lead to post-traumatic stress disorder.	These findings <u>**clearly**</u> indicate that.... These measures are <u>indeed</u> capable of improving the rates of economic recovery. The peak has <u>**obviously**</u> been reached for the market.
Nouns and Noun Phrases	
The rates could fall as much as 40%, but the <u>**estimate**</u>, admittedly, contains a significant margin of error. Based on this <u>**assumption**</u>... Our <u>**suggestion**</u> is...	Statistics point to <u>**the fact that**</u> France has... We have come to <u>**the conclusion that**</u> the gender differences in the use of hedges and boosters are minimal. Usually, a high level of <u>**certainty**</u> is required to have a diagnosis of DVT.

PRACTICE 3.4-B

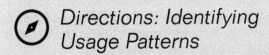 *Directions: Identifying
Usage Patterns*

In this exercise, you will explore the role that softening and/or boosting play in making writing credible and in distinguishing facts from information that is not yet proven. The passage below is an excerpt from:

Leman, J. (2020, January 16). *Is there a hidden 'super-earth' exoplanet orbiting our closest stellar neighbor?* www.popularmechanics .com/space/deep-space/a30547694/proxima-c-exoplanet/. Reprinted with permission.

- Read the passage carefully.
- Circle (or list) all softening words and boosters, including modals, adjectives, adverbs, or any other structures that you think contribute to strengthening or softening the author's claims.
- Discuss with a partner or group the reasons the author may have used these softening or boosting devices at these particular points.
  Example:
  The red dwarf star Proxima Centauri is our closest stellar neighbor; the star system is a measly 4.2 light years from Earth and <u>***can***</u> be seen with the naked eye. →
  (Without softening) The red dwarf star Proxima Centauri is our closest stellar neighbor; the star system is a measly 4.2 light years from Earth and **is** seen with the naked eye.
  Reason: *The sentence without "can" is too absolute. Not everyone can see the star with a naked eye, so it makes the author less credible.*
- Share your insights with the class.

The red dwarf star Proxima Centauri is our closest stellar neighbor; the star system is a measly 4.2 light years from Earth and can be seen with the naked eye. Because of this proximity, the system has long been a target of scientific inquiry and intrigue. In 2016, researchers discovered Proxima b, which has a mass similar to Earth's and an orbital period of 11 days, within the star system's habitable zone.

Even though it has been found in the habitable zone—that planetary sweet spot where experts believe liquid water could exist—Proxima b is tidally locked, meaning only one side of the planet faces its sun. Now, there's a new exoplanet candidate in town: Proxima c. Evidence suggests that it has a mass roughly six times that of Earth and orbits

its star once every 5 years, according to a research published Jan. 15 in the journal *Science Advances*.

But because Proxima Centauri is a relatively dim star, Proxima c is likely to be an extremely frigid world. Temperatures on the planet could dip as low as -388 degrees Fahrenheit, Space.com reports. It's unlikely we'd find life on such a chilly world.

Softening expressions:

_____
_____
_____
_____
_____
_____

Boosters:

_____
_____
_____
_____
_____
_____

PRACTICE 3.4-C

 Directions: Editing

The purpose of this exercise is for you to practice editing statements that are too weak and, therefore, not convincing or, conversely, too sweeping in their claims. Add, remove, or replace softening and boosting words to make the statements more accurate and credible. There is no one specific correct revision for each sentence. Multiple versions are possible. Discuss different possibilities and their effects on the sentences' persuasiveness.

1. All actors experience stage fright. Stage fright is a natural body reaction when the actor's muscles tense up and the activity of endocrine glands increases.

     _____
     _____
     _____
     _____

2. Mechanical engineering is the broadest type of engineering of all.

     _____
     _____
     _____
     _____

3. A mechanical engineer's job is to minimize the number of deaths or to prevent accidents from happening. The way that a mechanical engineer might go about doing this job is by trying to recreate the problem and what caused the accident then try to identify the best possible solution for this problem.

     _____
     _____
     _____
     _____

4. A negative effect that consumption of beef has on the human body is the contamination with dioxin. Dioxin is a toxic chemical which is found in any substance from the soil to the water systems.

     _____
     _____
     _____
     _____

5. Procrastination is the main problem college students face in achieving good grades. A responsible person may not procrastinate but may plan their work in advance and complete it ahead of time.

     _____
     _____
     _____
     _____

6. The main goal of sustainability in the landscape industry would be the idea of water conservation.

     _____
     _____
     _____
     _____

PRACTICE 3.4-D

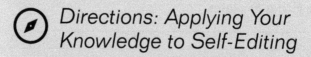 Directions: Applying Your Knowledge to Self-Editing

Now, it is your turn. Select a piece of your own writing approximately 300–500 words long. It can be an excerpt from an essay, a lab report, a case study, or a research paper – and edit it for the strength of your claims.

- Read your work one time through to remind yourself of your argument and supporting points.
- Read your work again, this time highlighting all markers of stance – modals, adjectives, adverbs, or nouns.
- Consider the appropriateness of these stance markers: Are they strong enough to demonstrate your confidence in what you are trying to say? Do they help you mitigate sweeping or unproven claims and avoid overstatements as appropriate?
- Revise, add, or remove softening and boosting language where necessary.

3.5 HOW CAN I USE VERBS TO EMPHASIZE SPECIFIC ASPECTS OF MY MESSAGE?

As writers, we make choices to emphasize different ideas to guide others to the aspects we think are most important. Depending on why we are writing, what kind of context we are writing in, and who we are writing to, we may focus on the actions, the people or entities that complete the action, or on the ones receiving the action. One basic but important way that we change the focus is through the order of words in the sentence.

The default order of words in the sentence (called "active voice") includes the people or entity that perform the action followed by the verb and any other necessary information for a complete idea.

Example: The **committee** **is considering** the new bill for tax-funded college tuition.

In some situations, writers want to change the focus from who or what is completing the action (in this example, the committee), so we change the order into what is called "passive voice."

Example: **The new bill** for tax-funded college tuition **is being considered** by the committee.

Example: **The new bill** for tax-funded college tuition **is being considered** this year.

As you can see, whoever or whatever receives the action (in this case, the new bill) moves to the front of the sentence, the verb changes slightly, and the people or entity completing the action are moved after the verb (with *by*) or removed completely. You can also see how this change shifts our focus as readers from the committee to the new bill.

After you work through this section of the chapter, you will be well on your way to say confidently:

◎ I can identify when writers use passive voice and determine why they make that choice.

◎ I can consider my contexts and purposes to decide when to use passive voice in my writing.

◎ I can proofread my own writing to ensure I use passive voice correctly, appropriately, and intentionally.

PRACTICE 3.5-A

 Directions: Identifying Usage Patterns

The purpose of this exercise is for you to identify when the writer uses passive voice. The excerpt comes from an essay written to highlight cultural differences. For each bolded verb, write whether the idea is passive voice (PV) or not passive voice (NPV). The first one is completed for you.

To identify whether the writer uses passive voice, use the following tricks:

* Find the verb, and ask yourself, "Who or what [verb]?" For example, for the first bolded verb below, you would ask, "Who or what arrived?" if the answer comes before the verb (in this case, basketball arrived), the writer is not using passive voice in that idea. If the answer does not come before the verb, you may find "who or what" completed the action later in the sentence (after *by*), or you may not know the answer. If that is the case, the writer is using passive voice for that idea. Be aware that for some verbs, (like am/is/are/was/were), you may need to include more information in your question so it makes sense. For example, in number 4 below, instead of "Who or what were?" you could ask, "Who or what were slats of wood?"
* To identify which ideas are in passive voice, add "by mermaids" after the verb. If the idea makes sense grammatically, the writer is using passive voice in that idea. If it doesn't make sense grammatically, the idea is not in passive voice.

Example: Basketball **arrived** *(by athletes)* in my village just one year before me.
Result: The idea doesn't make sense grammatically, so the writer is not using passive voice.
Example: Basketball **was introduced** *(by athletes)* in my village just one year before I arrived.
Result: The idea does make sense grammatically, so the writer is using passive voice.

From: Wesch, M. (2021). *The art of being human: A textbook for cultural anthropology.* New Prairie Press. Full text available for free at http://anth101.com/book/. Reprinted with the permission of the copyright holder.

Basketball (1) **arrived** in my village just one year before me. Large groups of all	1. NPV
ages (2) **gathered** every afternoon on a dirt court that	2.
(3) **had been cleared** of grass and pounded flat by nothing but bare human feet.	3.
The backboards (4) **were** slats of wood carved with axes from the surrounding	4.
forest, and the rims (5) **were made** of thick metal wire, salvaged from some	5.
other project. They (6) **played** every day until sundown, the perfect end to a day	6.
of gardening and gathering firewood. It was a welcome and familiar sight, and I	
eagerly (7) **joined** in.	7.
I (8) **stepped** onto the court and	8.
(9) **noticed** that for the first time in my life, I	9.
(10) **was** taller than everybody else. Even better, the rims	10.
(11) **had been set** to about 8 feet, perfect for dunking. I	11.
(12) **rushed** in for a massive dunk on my first opportunity,	12.
putting my team up 6-0. I (13) **looked** to my friend	13.
Kodenim for a high five, but he (14) **looked** concerned	14.
or even angry as he (15) **slapped** his	15.
hand to his forearm as if to say, "Foul! Foul!"	
I (16) **owned** the court. I	16.
(17) **grabbed** a steal and went in for another dunk, looking to Kodenim again for	17.
a fist pump or cheer. Instead, he (18) **gave** me a stern look and pounded his bicep	18.
with his hand. He (19) **was trying** to send me a signal,	19.
but I (20) **wasn't getting** it.	20.
Later I (21) **would find out** that he was trying to send me a not-so subtle reminder	21.
of the score. Rather than a "Base 10" counting system (cycling 1-10 then starting	
again 11-20 and so on), the villagers (22) **use** a "Base 27" system and use their	22.
entire upper body to count it. Numbers 1-5 (23) **are** on the hand, 6-10 along the	23.
arm, 11 at the neck, 12 is the ear, 13 the eye, 14 the nose, and then back down the	
other side. 6-0, Kodenim (24) **slaps** his forearm. 8-0, he slaps his bicep.	24.
It is a clever system that (25) **suits** them well. There are no annual seasons to track	25.
in Papua New Guinea, so the most relevant natural cycle to track is not the path of	
the sun, but the path of the moon. A hunter (26) **can start counting** from the new	26.
moon and know that as the count (27) **gets** closer to his eyes (days 13, 14, and 15)	27.
he (28) **will be able to see** at night using the light of the full moon.	28.
Women (29) **can use** it to count the days until their next menstrual cycle.	29.
I (30) **drifted** into the background of the game as I tried to figure out what was	30.
going on. The other team (31) **started** scoring until the	31.
game (32) **was tied** at 14. "14-14!" the score keeper	32.
(33) **announced** with jubilation, pointing to his nose. Everybody	33.
(34) **cheered** and **walked** off the court. Where's everybody going? I	34.
thought. The game (35) **is tied up**. "Next basket	35.
(36) **wins**!" I suggested. Kodenim	36.
(37) **took** me aside. "Mike, we	37.
(38) **like** to end in a tie," he said, and then he	38.
(39) **smiled** the way you smile at a four-year-old who	39.
(40) **is** just **learning** the ways of the world, and gently	40.
recommended that I not do any more dunking. "People might be jealous."	

Directions: Identifying Meaning

The purpose of this exercise is for you to notice why the writer uses passive voice.

- Reread the passage above, and for each verb that you marked as passive voice (PV) explain why the writer changed the focus in that idea:
  - to emphasize who or what receives the action
  - to emphasize the action
  - to de-emphasize who or what completed the action
- or to remove who or what completed the action.

 ## SUMMARY: FUNCTION AND FORMS OF PASSIVE VOICE

Reasons for Choosing Passive Voice	Example
Who or what completed the action is unknown, irrelevant, or obvious	• The circular pattern of massive upright stones at the mysterious Stonehenge **was built** over a period of 1500 years. • Individuals in Generation Z **were born** between the mid-to-late 1990s and the early 2010s. • The New York City Marathon **has been run** every year since 1970, with two exceptions.
To emphasize actions and results instead of who or what performed the actions	• The New York City Marathon **was cancelled** in 2012 due to the landfall of Hurricane Sandy and in 2020 due to the COVID-19 pandemic. • Our core ideas and ideals **are constructed** by the cultures we are raised in.
To show objectivity by implying that the results will be the same, regardless of who performs the actions	• Participants in the study **were asked** to respond to a series of questions. • The solution **was heated** to 90°C for approximately 30 minutes and then allowed to cool.
To shift blame or responsibility (at times intentionally not identifying who or what completed the action)	• The marketing **wasn't completed** with enough lead time before the products hit the shelves. • The concept of money bail **was established** to give the accused an incentive to return to court, but it has become a system of "wealth-based incarceration"

Passive voice is not always the best choice, which is why it is not our default usage. At times, passive voice can make an idea more confusing or less clear, so be aware of the expectations of the people you are communicating with. There are also verbs that cannot be used in passive voice (such as *belong*. "Something is belonged" is ungrammatical and nonsensical). Even when passive voice is an effective choice, it is usually used in combination with the default active voice.

Passive voice can be used in any time frame, but it always includes some form of a *be* verb (am, is, are, was, were, being, been) followed by a verb with an -en or -ed ending. See section 3.1 for a review of the time frame meaning and uses.

Form	Example
am/is/are + verb with -en or -ed	We have put so much plastic into our environment that single-use plastic products **are** now **found** in our drinking water, our seafood, and even our sea salt.
am/is/are/was/were being + verb with -en or -ed	Less than 10 percent of disposable plastics **is being recycled**, so much of the plastic that is put in recycling bins ends up in landfills, incinerators, or waterways.
was/were + verb with -en or -ed	Single-use plastics **were used** sparingly until the low-cost production made them cheap and common.
have/has/had been + verb with -en or -ed	Legislation to reduce straws, bags, and other single-use plastics **has been adopted** by cities, states, and countries.
can/could/should/will/ would/may/ must/might be + verb with -en or -ed	The amount of plastic in our ocean is projected to double in the next 12 years, but this projection **can be stopped** if we change our reliance on plastic.

PRACTICE 3.5-B

 Directions: Comparison

The purpose of this exercise is for you to understand and explain the differences in meaning between passages that use passive voice and those that omit passive voice.

• Read both passages carefully. Passage 1 contains ideas in passive voice, which are bolded. Passage 2 is the same paragraph, but it is edited to remove all of the passive voice.

• Then, discuss the passages with a partner:

  • Compare the two passages in their style and impact on the reader
  • Explain how the meaning and the effects on the reader differ between the two
  • Use the reasons in the summary above to help you identify why the writer used passive voice.

Passage 1

From: Bennett, Jeannette, "Advertising Dollars and Decisions," *Page One Economics*, April 2017, Federal Reserve Bank of St. Louis, https://research.stlouisfed.org/publications/page1-econ/2017-04-03/advertising-dollars-and-decisions[3]

> Having dollars in your pocket is one thing; keeping them there is another. With so many businesses selling goods and services, there is a lot of competition in the marketplace for the money in your pocket. In fact, consumers **are bombarded** with as many as 4,000 to 10,000 advertisements each day! This advertising **is designed** to increase or create demand for products by influencing consumers' choices about spending. Through persuasion, some dollars in your pocket **are spent** because of advertising.

Passage 2

> Having dollars in your pocket is one thing; keeping them there is another. With so many businesses selling goods and services, there is a lot of competition in the marketplace for the money in your pocket. In fact, advertisers **bombard** consumers with as many as 4,000 to 10,000 advertisements each day! The advertisers **design** the ads to

increase or create demand for products by influencing consumers' choices about spending. Through persuasion, you **spend** some dollars in your pocket because of advertising.

PRACTICE 3.5-C

 Directions: Editing

In this exercise, you will hone your editing skills, focusing on correcting errors in passive voice form and in choosing active or passive voice.

- Read the passage below first to get its general idea.
- Decide whether the use of the passive voice or active voice is appropriate in each case. Change the verb forms where necessary.
- Add, remove, switch, or replace words or word endings to use the correct passive voice form when appropriate.

Biometrics, which are physical characteristics and measurements (like fingerprints), can be use to identify individuals. Most of us are familiar with the use of facial recognition when we tag photos on social media and when law enforcement analyzes images to identify suspects or witnesses, and more and more commonly, biometrics are being use to protect sensitive information or access. Because these physical characteristics like facial structure, voice, and even irises in our eyes are relatively individualized and rarely change, biometrics are replaced or supplementing password protection in personal and business settings. With the vast amount of sign-in information we are required to have, many of us are relied on weak or repeated passwords for many different sites. In these cases, our accounts can hacked much more easily than the sites that use biometric sign-in credentials.

PRACTICE 3.5-D

 Directions: Drawing Conclusions

The goal of this practice is to identify contexts for appropriately using passive voice so that you can make effective choices in your writing. Answer the questions below and discuss with a partner or small group.

Question	Answer
This chapter section includes passages and examples from many different fields of study and kinds of writing. Using the examples to support your conclusions, **explain** which contexts use passive voice more commonly. Consider whether passive voice is more common in fields of study or topics that are more data-driven or more human-focused. (Be sure to include in your consideration the major and career fields that may be in your future.)	
Explain why you think passive voice is more common in the contexts that you identified above. Do not stop at one reason and be specific. Provide examples to support your position.	
From the passages and examples included in this chapter, how commonly do you think passive voice is used in general in writing? Explain.	

PRACTICE 3.5-F

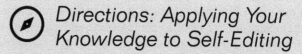 *Directions: Applying Your Knowledge to Self-Editing*

The ultimate goal of all of these practices is to improve your writing, so this practice asks you to apply what you have learned to your essays and reports. Choose one writing assignment that is currently in progress and edit your draft to identify appropriate and correct usage of passive voice.

NOTES

1 Carlson, W. E. (2017, June 20). The history of early computing technology. Computer Graphics and Computer Animation: A Retrospective Overview. Pressbooks. https://ohiostate.pressbooks.pub/graphicshistory/chapter/the -history-of-early-computing-technology/

2 All Esri excerpts are the intellectual property of Esri and are used herein with permission. Copyright © 2021 Esri and its licensors. All rights reserved.

3 This citation format is specified by the copyright holder, Federal Reserve Bank of St. Louis. Reprinted with permission.

 **4**
Noun Groups
Tools for Complex Reading and Writing

Prepare to be shocked – a noun is *not* a person, place, or thing. In fact, in English, most of the time, we indicate places through phrases beginning with prepositions – those short words, like *in, on,* or *at*: *on the shelf, in the book, at the airport.* The words *shelf, book,* or *airport* are, indeed, nouns because they refer to things, but to indicate a place, all of them need a preposition in front of them. So that leaves us with nouns being words for just persons and things. Kind of basic, right? Well, no, not exactly. There is so much more to nouns than that!

Nouns also refer to ideas, phenomena (the singular form of which is *phenomenon*), and even actions we describe, explain, discuss, or argue for or against when we speak or write. As such, nouns are the main carriers of information in a text. Furthermore, nouns also act as magnets for other words, attracting all kinds of modifiers that allow academic and workplace writers to condense as much information as possible into as few words as possible while remaining clear and transparent to their readers. These clusters of modifiers gathered around a noun are called noun phrases or, less formally, **noun groups**. In this book, we will use the term "**noun groups.**" Look at this sentence:

> The **<u>aim</u>** *of the present* **<u>study</u>** *was to describe and compare* **physical <u>profiles</u>** *and* **certain psychological <u>aspects</u>** *of sitting* **<u>volleyball</u> <u>players</u>** *in a* **national <u>team</u>** *and in a* **<u>league</u> <u>team</u>**.[1]

All the underlined words in it are nouns, and the words in the bold-faced font are their modifiers. Note that nouns can even be modifiers for other nouns, like in a phrase "*volleyball players*", where the noun *volleyball* specifies what kind of sport the *players* are playing. Noun groups in this example sentence constitute two thirds of the whole content!

DOI: 10.4324/9781003159889-5

Nouns also make up the core of set phrases we often use in persuasive and informative writing: *the **fact** that, as a **matter** of **fact**, in **addition** to, the **idea** that,* and so on, and so forth.

No wonder nouns are important for clear, concise, and informative writing!

In this chapter, you will learn how to use nouns and noun groups effectively by:

- Becoming familiar with the patterns of using *a, an, the,* and similar words that specify noun meanings
- Developing skills in building complex yet clear noun groups to convey information
- Identifying the most efficient ways of using nouns for general statements
- Editing your work for clear references

This chapter consists of four sections, each of which addresses a separate skill from the list above:

4.1   Nouns and their determiners
4.2   Noun groups in academic and workplace writing
4.3   Nouns for making generalizations
4.4   Pronouns and their referents

4.1 WHICH NOUNS CAN BE PLURAL? WHEN DO NOUNS NEED *A*, *AN*, OR *THE*?

After you work through this section of the chapter, you will be well on the way to say confidently:

- 🎯 I know which nouns can be used in the plural form and which ones cannot.

- 🎯 I know how to use the words *a/an* and *the* (also known as determiners) that come with nouns.

PRACTICE 4.1-A

 Directions: Identifying Usage Patterns

The purpose of this exercise is to draw your attention to how determiners – words like *a*, *an*, or *the* – are used before nouns.

- Read the passage below and put the words *a*, *an*, or *the* in the blanks in the sentences. If none of these words fit well to make sense, write ∅ in the blank.
- The first sentence is marked for you as an example.
- **In some blanks, more than one choice is possible.** Discuss your results with a classmate and compare your choices.
- Then answer the questions below the text.

Text:

From: Ferracioli, L. (May 8, 2020). For a child, being carefree is intrinsic to a well-lived life. *AEON Media Group Ltd.* Retrieved from https://aeon.co/ideas/for-a-child-being-carefree-is-intrinsic -to-a-well-lived-life on March 24, 2021. Reprinted under Creative Commons License.

(1) Some people are lucky enough to look back at their childhood with ∅ affection for *a* time in life without much stress and

anxiety. (2) They might think of _____ long hours spent playing in _____ backyard free of _____ worry or pursuing _____ projects and _____ relationships without _____ apprehension or _____ fear. (3) Such tender memories are often in stark contrast to _____ lives many lead as _____ adults, where _____ stress and _____ anxiety seem to dominate.

(4) _____ fact that many people struggle to be carefree in _____ adulthood raises a number of interesting questions about _____ relationship between _____ carefreeness and _____ good life. (5) Is being carefree _____ special good of _____ childhood? (6) Is it something that confers _____ meaning on _____ life of a child, without doing the same for adults? (7) Or do adults need to be more carefree, and so be more like children, in order for their lives to go well? (8) Most importantly, if carefreeness is indeed _____ necessary precondition for _____ good life, why exactly is that so?

(9) As _____ parent of two young children, and someone who works on family philosophy, I have recently turned my attention to _____ question of what it means for childhoods to go well. (10) Thinking about the goods of parental love and education, I have realized that there is something special about being carefree that makes it _____ necessary component of _____ well-lived childhood. (11) Yet when it comes to adults, I have found that some can lead wonderful, meaningful lives without being carefree.

Comparisons

1. Were there some sentences or blanks where you and your classmates made different choices, e.g., one person chose *a/an* and another person *the*, or one person chose *the*, and another ∅? If yes, what are these sentences? List the sentences and choices in the table below or on a separate sheet of paper. **The table provides for two choices, but keep in mind that more is also possible.** The first sentence is included as an example.

Sentence Number	Choice 1	Choice 2
1	...a time in life	... the time in life

2. Are there differences in the shades of meaning between these choices? If yes, what are they?

   Example: *"...a time in life" sounds like childhood can be one of many times without stress and anxiety, and "...the time in life" sounds like childhood is the only such time. The choice between "a" and "the" depends on how the writer feels about the times in their life that they didn't feel stress and anxiety – only when they were a child, or many other times too.*

   _____
   _____
   _____
   _____
   _____
   _____
   _____
   _____

SUMMARY: CHOOSING THE RIGHT LITTLE WORDS (DETERMINERS)

The words **a** (or its variation **an** before words that begin with vowel sounds) and **the** are some of the most frequent words in the English language. Their job is to indicate to the reader whether the writer is referring to one thing of many similar things (**a/an**) or a specific thing already known to the audience (**the**). As a result, these words can make an important difference in how the readers will understand the writer's points. Compare these sentences:

> <u>*A*</u> *study published in Germany found that people consume at least 50,000 microplastic particles per year.*
>
> <u>*The*</u> *study published in Germany found that people consume at least 50,000 microplastic particles per year.*

The first sentence suggests that we, as readers, are not expected to know anything about this study yet. It is one of many studies conducted by multiple researchers on multiple issues. The information about this study is new to us. It is just being introduced for the first time. Maybe we will learn about this study in the paragraph that follows this sentence.

The second sentence sounds like it's been taken out of a text that already told us something about this study or we are supposed to know about it from some other source.

Both sentences are perfectly grammatically correct, but they show that their authors have different expectations of what the readers already know, and what they don't yet know.

SUMMARY: HOW TO USE
A/AN AND *THE*

THE		A / AN or NOTHING	
The reader knows which *specific thing or concept* the writer is talking about.		*The reader does not know* which specific thing or concept the writer is talking about.	
Already mentioned	**Culturally shared or easily identifiable in context**	**New to the reader**	**Random, non-specific, or one of many**
"Everybody feelin' good?" *Neil Young* asked the full house Saturday night at the Pantages Theatre… "We'll find out," *the rock god* responded as he took a seat surrounded by six acoustic guitars, three pianos, a banjo, pump organ and an array of har-monicas.[2] In June, a study found that people eat at least 50,000 *microplastic particles* per year; research has also found *the particles* in cancerous human lung tissue.[3]	Some people might think of long hours spent playing in *the backyard* free of worry. *The Superdome* is known for being noisy, but *the fans* have taken it to another level for the N.F.C. championship game.[4] US students test below *the students in other developed countries* in math and science.[5]	In June, *a study* found that people eat at least 50,000 microplastic particles per year; research has also found the particles in cancerous human lung tissue.[6] If more *evidence* was needed that we desperately have to curb our dependence on plastic, ASAP, *researchers* have found *large amounts of microplastic* frozen deep in Arctic ice floes.[3]	"Everybody feelin' good?" Neil Young asked the full house Saturday night at the Pantages Theatre. "How are you feelin'?" shouted *a fan.*[2] *A fifth-generation Texan*, Bob earned *a bachelor's degree* from Harvard University. He covers Gov. Greg Abbott, the state budget, *school textbooks,* and *child welfare.*[7]

PRACTICE 4.1-B

  Directions: Identifying Meaning

In this exercise, you will consider the reasons why an author may choose *a/an, the,* or no determiner at all with a particular noun group.

- Read the following text carefully and then think about each underlined noun group.

> • Write the reason for the choice of *a/an, the,* or "no determiner"
>   (or ∅) in the column next to the text as follows:
>   A. the information has been mentioned before (the)
>   B. somebody or something unique (the)
>   C. all of the things or people in a particular category (the)
>   D. one or some (not all) of many similar, generic things or
>   people (a, an, or nothing/∅)
>   E. information is new to the reader (a, an, or nothing/∅)
> • The first question is done for you as an example.

Excerpt from: *Mary Todd Lincoln,* © White House Historical
Association. Reprinted with permission.

Mary Todd Lincoln	Reason
As (1) ___ girlhood companion remembered her, Mary Todd was vivacious and impulsive, with (2) interesting personality—but "she now and then could not restrain a witty, sarcastic speech that cut deeper than she intended..." A young lawyer summed her up in 1840: "the very creature of excitement." All of these attributes marked her life, bringing her both (3) ____ happiness and tragedy.	(1) _E_ (2) ____ (3) ____
She was born on December 13, 1818, to Eliza Parker and Robert Smith Todd, pioneer settlers of Kentucky. Mary lost her mother before (4) ___ age of seven. Her father remarried; and Mary remembered her childhood as "desolate" although she belonged to (5) ____ aristocracy of Lexington, with high-spirited social life and a sound private education.	(4) ____ (5) ____
When she was nearly 21, she went to Springfield, Illinois, to live with her sister Elizabeth Todd Edwards. Here she met Abraham Lincoln—in his own words, "a poor nobody then." Three years later, after (6) ____ stormy courtship and broken engagement, they were married. Though opposites in background and temperament, they were united by an enduring love and Mary's confidence in her husband's ability and his gentle consideration of her excitable ways.	(6) ____
Their years in Springfield brought (7) ___hard work, a family of boys, and reduced circumstances to (8) ____ pleasure-loving girl who had never felt responsibility before. Lincoln's single term in Congress (1847–49), gave Mary and (9) ____ boys a winter in Washington, but scant opportunity for social life. Finally, her unwavering faith in her husband won ample justification with his election as president in 1860.	(7) ____ (8) ____ (9) ____

SUMMARY: COUNT AND NONCOUNT NOUNS

English nouns can be divided into two groups:

Count Nouns	Noncount Nouns

• Nouns that refer to things or concepts that can be counted:
  • One study, two studie<u>s</u>
  • One backyard, many backyard<u>s</u>
  • One Texan, 29 million Texan<u>s</u>
  • One assignment, multiple assignment<u>s</u>
• These nouns typically change between singular and plural forms with the addition of an -s or -es at the end, but there are exceptions.
  • One fish, two fish
  • One person, 300 people
  • One life, several lives
  • One woman, many women
  • One nucleus, multiple nuclei
These nouns are called **count nouns**.
	• Nouns that can be measured, but not counted:
	  • A little research, a lot of research, but not "two researches"
	  • Little welfare, a large amount of welfare, but not "several welfares"
	  • Some evidence, abundant evidence, but not "many evidences"
	  • Little homework, a lot of homework, but not "a few homeworks"
	These nouns are called **noncount nouns.** You may also see them referred to as **mass nouns.**

Singular count nouns always have to have a determiner in front of them: • **The <u>wife</u> of the <u>president</u>** • **A** childhood **<u>companion</u>** • **Her** girlhood **<u>companion</u>** • **That** particular **<u>problem</u>**	Non-count nouns are special: • You cannot add an -s to a noncount noun to make it plural. • You cannot use *a* or *an* in front of a noncount noun.
Exception	
Some nouns can switch between their count and noncount forms depending on whether they refer to things that can be counted or things that can be measured: • Things that drive people to drink *<u>a lot of coffee</u>* may also cause other changes in diet.[8] (non-count; "coffee" as measurable liquid) • She paid for *<u>two coffees</u>* and a donut. (count; "a coffee" = "a cup of coffee")	

SUMMARY: OTHER LITTLE WORDS (DETERMINERS)

Words that often take the place of a/an or the	Examples
Words that show **belonging or possession**:	My, your, his, her, our, their, its (home) The student's (notebook), Jenna's (car), passengers' (luggage)
Numbers:	One, two, three... (apples) First, second, third... (house)
Words that show **measure or amount**:	Some, several, each, every, a few... (students/houses/apples) Each/every (student/house/apple)
Words that show **closeness or distance**:	That, this (apple) Those/these (houses)

PRACTICE 4.1-C

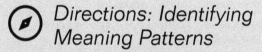

Directions: Identifying Meaning Patterns

In this exercise, you will practice identifying whether a particular noun is used as a count one or a noncount one. The decision tree below should help you in your identification.

- First, read the passage below carefully to get the general idea of the text. This is a passage from Charles Dickens's short story *Hunted Down*, published for the first time in 1860.
- Some nouns in it – not all – have been underlined. Look at each underlined noun carefully. Follow the steps in the decision tree. Then mark (C) for count nouns and (NC) for non-count nouns.
- You will find that some nouns do not fit the pattern of deciding which nouns are count and which ones are not. Highlight these nouns and discuss with your classmates why you think they do not follow the pattern. The nouns in the first sentence have been marked for you as an example.

From: Dickens, C. (1860). *Hunted down*. Retrieved from Project Gutenberg: www.gutenberg.org/files/807/807-h/807-h.htm.

Decision Tree

Text

The partition which separated my own office from our general outer office in the City was of thick (1) **plate-glass** (NC). I could see through it what passed in the outer office, without hearing a (2) **word** (C). I had it put up in place of a wall that had been there for years,—ever since the house was built. It is no matter whether I did or did not make the (3) **change** in order that I might derive my first impression of strangers, who came to us on (4) **business**, from their faces alone, without being influenced by anything they said. Enough to mention that I turned my glass (5) **partition** to that account, and that a Life Assurance Office is at all times exposed to be practised upon by the most crafty and cruel of the human race.

It was through my glass partition that I first saw the (6) **gentleman** whose story I am going to tell.

He had come in without my observing it, and had put his hat and umbrella on the broad (7) **counter**, and was bending over it to take some (8) **papers** from one of the clerks. He was about forty or so, dark, exceedingly well dressed in black,—being in (9) **mourning**,—and the hand he extended with a polite (10) **air**, had a particularly well-fitting black-kid (11) **glove** upon it. His (12) **hair**, which was elaborately brushed and oiled, was parted straight up the middle; and he presented this parting to the clerk, exactly (to my thinking) as if he had said, in so many words: 'You must take me, if you please, my (13) **friend**, just as I show myself. Come straight up here, follow the gravel path, keep off the (14) **grass**, I allow no trespassing.'

PRACTICE 4.1-D

 Directions: Editing

In this exercise, you will practice applying the knowledge and skills you've gained in the preceding exercises. The goal is to practice using *a*, *an*, and *the* with appropriate nouns.

- The passage below has been adapted from an undergraduate research paper. Read it carefully first.
- Some sentences in the passage contain inaccuracies and not always appropriate choices in the use of *a*, *the*, and plural and singular noun forms. Your task is to **identify and correct them.**
- In the first sentence, the problems are identified, corrected, and explained as an example for you. In the second sentence, the area where there may be a problem is underlined, but it is up to you to correct it and explain why it needs correction. From the third sentence on, you will need to **find the potential inaccuracies, provide better choices, and explain them on your own.**
- It is useful to do this exercise with a partner or two.
- Remember: there may be more than one appropriate choice for some noun groups, even though the meanings these choices convey may be slightly different. Discuss such differences with a partner.

Student Text	Explanations
A few weeks ago, when I asked a stranger what came to mind when he thought of "food science", his response *an* *a* was ~~a~~ image of ~~the~~ mad scientist inventing new foods. In reality, food science is <u>**multidisciplinary study**</u> of foods by applying chemistry, biology, and physics to develop better ways of creating, preserving, and delivering foods to people. Food scientists not only invent new foods but also help improve quality of food so that the health and well-being of the person increases as he or she can choose a variety of foods to eat. Food seems to be easily obtained in the United States but unfortunately, a global food security is a big problem. The food security is defined as people having access to foods at all times so that they can maintain a healthy lifestyle. The food security is built upon three pillars: food availability, food access, and food use. These three pillars are used to define all levels of the food security from the household to the nation. Lack of a global food security is one of the biggest fears mankind faces today. The food scientists of the twenty-first century will need to help improve the food supply or to find alternatives and substitutes should the Earth run out of its natural resources.	*"An image" – the word "image" begins with a vowel sound, so "a" needs to change to "an."* *"a mad scientist" – there is no specific mad scientist that the reader knows about here. It's just a random mad scientist.*

4.2 WHICH NOUN GROUPS SHOULD I USE IN ACADEMIC AND WORKPLACE WRITING?

After you work through this section of the chapter, you will be well on the way to say confidently:

🎯 I know how to package a lot of information into clear and compact noun groups.

PRACTICE 4.2-A

 Directions: Identifying Usage Patterns

The aim of this exercise is to draw your attention to how noun groups are built and what kind of modifiers they can take to incorporate important information into each group. Most (although not all) noun groups in this text have been marked in a bold-faced font, and the main nouns in each group have been underlined.

- First, read the text through to understand its main idea.
- Second, examine each bold-faced noun group and determine what it is made up of: What is the main noun, and what are its modifiers?
- Third, write this group in the table below in the appropriate section of the table. An example of each noun group type has been provided in the table.

From: Wikibooks (2021, April 19). *New Zealand history/Polynesian settlement.* https://en.wikibooks.org/wiki/New_Zealand_History /Polynesian_Settlement. Licensed under Creative Commons Attribution-Share Alike License.

Text

Polynesian Settlement of New Zealand

Around 950 AD, it is believed **Polynesian** <u>settlers</u> used **subtropical weather** <u>systems</u>, **star** <u>constellations</u>, **water** <u>currents</u>, and **animal** <u>migration</u> to find **their** <u>way</u> from **their native** <u>islands</u> in central

Polynesia to <u>New Zealand</u>. As **the** <u>settlers</u> colonized **the** <u>country</u>, they developed **their distinctive Maori** <u>culture</u>.

According to <u>Maori</u>, **the first Polynesian** <u>explorer</u> **to reach New** Zealand was <u>Kupe</u>, **who traveled across the Pacific in a Polynesian-style voyaging canoe**. It is thought <u>Kupe</u> reached <u>New Zealand</u> at <u>Hokianga Harbour</u>, in Northland, about **1070** <u>years</u> ago.

Although there has been **much** <u>debate</u> **about when and how Polynesians actually started settling New Zealand**, the **current** <u>understanding</u> is that they migrated from **east and central Polynesia, the Southern Cook and Society islands** <u>region</u>. They migrated deliberately, at **different** <u>times</u>, in **different** <u>canoes</u>, first arriving in New Zealand in **the late 10th** <u>century</u>.

For **a long** <u>time</u> **during the nineteenth and twentieth centuries**, it was believed **the first** <u>inhabitants</u> of New Zealand were the Maori people, who hunted **giant** <u>birds</u> called moas. The theory then established **the idea that the Maori people migrated from Polynesia in a Great Fleet and took New Zealand from the Moriori**, establishing **an agricultural** <u>society</u>. However, **new** <u>evidence</u> suggests that the Moriori were **a** <u>group</u> of mainland **Maori who migrated from New Zealand to the Chatham Islands**, developing **their own distinctive, peaceful** <u>culture</u>. There was also **another** <u>tribe</u> on the Chatham islands these were <u>Maori</u> **who migrated away from New Zealand**. They called themselves the Moriori. There were **a few skirmishes** and in the end, the Moriori were wiped out.

Types of Modifiers	Noun Groups from the Text
Adjective(s) + **Main Noun**	*Polynesian* <u>*settlers*</u>
Modifying Noun + **Main Noun**	*Star* <u>*constellations*</u>
Adjective(s) + Modifying Noun + **Main Noun**	*Their distinctive Maori* <u>*culture*</u>
Main Noun + Who/Which/That Clause	<u>*Kupe*</u>*, who traveled across the Pacific in a Polynesian-style voyaging canoe*
(Adjective(s)/ Modifying Noun +) **Main Noun** + to + Verb	*The first Polynesian* <u>*explorer*</u> *to reach New Zealand*
(Adjective(s)/ Modifying Noun +) **Main Noun** + Preposition + Another Noun Group	*A long* <u>*time*</u> *during the nineteenth and twentieth century*
(Adjective(s)/ Modifying Noun +) **Main Noun** + -ed/-ing verb	*Giant* <u>*birds*</u> *called moas*

PRACTICE 4.2-B

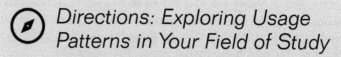

Directions: Exploring Usage Patterns in Your Field of Study

The purpose of this exercise is to identify how noun groups are used in your major, field of study, and/or work.

- Find a passage from a reading in your major or a publication related to your job. This can be a textbook from a major class, or a professional trade magazine or newsletter, or a research article. You may want to ask a professor in your major to point you to such a publication. Make sure that the passage is at least 200 words long.
- Underline all nouns in this passage and highlight the noun groups formed around these nouns.
- Examine each noun group and analyze its structure. Use the same table format as Practice 4.2-A above.
- Use the questions below to identify and discuss patterns you notice.
- Summarize your findings below.

Discussion Questions

- What types of noun groups are most common in texts in your field?
- What can you do in your own writing to imitate the style typical of your field?

Summarize Your Findings

- Write a short paragraph (three to four sentences) reflecting on what you've learned from analyzing a sample of writing in your major, field of study, or work and discussing the noun groups and patterns with classmates.

_____
_____
_____
_____
_____
_____
_____
_____
_____
_____

PRACTICE 4.2-C

> ### ⊘ Directions: Editing for Conciseness
>
> The goal of this exercise is to develop skills in building compact and informative noun groups.
>
> - Read each set of sentences and phrases provided in the exercises. They have been adapted – i.e., simplified – from published work (newspaper articles, research papers, blogs, and literature) or from student essays.
> - If possible, work with at least one partner or a group. Create at least two different ways to compress the information from the sentences and phrases into a single noun group. An example is provided for you.
> - Look back at the chart you filled in for Practice 4.2-B, in which you analyzed a text from your major. Try to identify the type of each noun group you create. Are they similar in structure to the noun groups in your field or different? Follow the example provided.
> - The new sentences you create will not have completely identical connotations – that is, overtones of meaning that result from the different arrangement of words. Discuss with your partners how the new sentences with complex noun groups differ from each other in the shades of meaning and nuance.

Example

Original:

The material is mixed into a <u>paint</u>. This paint <u>looks quite ordinary</u>. It is <u>applied in a single coat</u>.

Revisions:

Option 1: *The material is mixed into <u>ordinary-looking single-coat paint</u>. (Adjective + Modifying Noun + Main Noun)*

Option 2: *The material is mixed into <u>an ordinary-looking paint applied in a single coat</u>. (Adjective + Main Noun + -ed verb)*

Option 3: *This material is mixed into <u>a single-coat paint that looks quite ordinary</u>. (Modifying Noun + Main Noun + That-clause)*

1. Some physicists have conducted new research. These physicists work at Brown University and at the Massachusetts Institute of Technology. The research is fascinating. (Hint: There are two different noun groups you should create in new sentences.)

   _____

   _____

   _____

   _____

   _____

2. The size of your brain can change. One factor is the temperature that the air has. This is the air around you.

   _____

   _____

   _____

   _____

   _____

3. The mound is made of snow. It is little. It seems to have two eyes. The eyes are dark. The mound moves. It reveals a body. It is an arctic fox. The fox is alone. Its body is small and furry.

   _____

   _____

   _____

   _____

   _____

4. In this paper, I will discuss landscape design. This design is sustainable. It focuses on water conservation.

   _____

   _____

   _____

   _____

   _____

PRACTICE 4.2-D

 Directions: Practicing Writing Concisely

In this exercise, you will become familiar with the technique that workplace and academic writers often use to take whole sentences and turn them into compact noun groups that can be then used as parts of other sentences. This technique involves taking verbs and turning them into nouns or adjectives that modify nouns. This allows the writer to:

(a) Compress important information into as few words as possible without losing clarity

(b) Avoid repeating explanations that the reader already knows

(c) Present actions and processes as phenomena or things that can be examined and discussed.

- Read the text below. This is an excerpt from a trade publication in the field of Logistics and Operations Management.
- Examine all the underlined nouns and adjectives. **Determine which verb they were formed from and how.** Examples have been provided for you.

From: Morrison, B. (2021, April 18). Plant-based is the new organic, but look before you leap. *Foodlogistics.com*. Retrieved from: www .foodlogistics.com/sustainability/grocery-retail/article/21366117/ plantbased-is-the-new-organic-but-look-before-you-leap.

Text	Original Verb and the Noun or Adjective from the Text
### The Challenge of Entering the Plant-Based Food Market According to the International Food Information Council, taste is the primary **purchase driver** for all food products, and consumers were willing to pay more for it. However, **evolving** drivers, like **sustainability** and health benefits, are following closely behind the more traditional factors of taste and price. In fact, more than 50% of consumers are strongly motivated by these newer drivers.	*Purchase (verb) → purchase (noun)* *Drive (verb) → driver (noun)* *Evolve (verb) → evolving (adjective)*
New products need **differentiation** strategies to catch and retain consumers' attention. It can't be the same thing as **competing** products for the same price. Brands need to think through their **marketable** advantages and how to tell that story to consumers. What's more, the processes and technologies fueling this **growing** industry are still developing. **Plant-based substitutes** for **animal-based** **products** are relatively new, and **entrants** into this market should be prepared to invest significantly in **product** and **process development**. **Specialized equipment** and **co-packing** options, which are readily available for many conventional consumer **packaged** goods (CPGs), are less available for still **developing** **plant-based** **products**. Some may not yet exist.	

SUMMARY: WRITING MORE CONCISELY WITH NOUN GROUPS

Turning verbs into nouns and other elements of noun groups is an important skill in academic and workplace writing. It allows you to:

- Avoid repeating the same words or clauses
- Condense information into smaller texts
- Convey an objective stance in your writing.

The table below shows three ways you can turn verbs into noun groups or noun group components:

Strategy	Word Examples	Sentence Examples[9]
Turn a verb into a noun. Use the new noun as either the main one or the modifying one.	to analyze → analysis to increase → an increase to evolve → evolution to develop → development to propose → proposal	Due to rapid **advancement** in modern computer vision and traffic **surveillance** techniques, vehicle **detection techniques** at night based on image processing have gained much attention in recent years.
Use an -ing or -ed form of the verb as an adjective to describe the main noun	to enhance productivity → enhan**ced** productivity a body that governs → a govern**ing** body a tendency that grows → a grow**ing** tendency to modernize equipment → moderniz**ed** equipment	Unlike the U.S., however, the Japanese system is basing its total selection process on the basis of a test score rather than the **demonstrated ability** of a student in more than one endeavor. But most [respondents] had confidence in either the universality of human reason or the **transforming power** of free political institutions to make immigrants into Americans.
Create a -ing noun (aka gerund) from a verb	To implement new technology → implementing new technology To explore all viable options → exploring all viable options To digitize content → digitizing content	The new monetary policy was used to ensure long-term economic growth rather than a means of **temporary financing**. The first phase is designated for data collections and **data processing** to extract reliable information from the raw data.

PRACTICE 4.2-E

 Directions: Editing

In this exercise, you will be applying the skills of turning verb-based clauses into noun groups in order to make writing more concise, informative, and non-repetitive.

- The passages below are excerpts from typical student essays and research papers written for classes in a variety of majors, from Early Childhood Education, to Sociology, to Mechanical Engineering, to Hospitality Management. Read each passage carefully.
- Identify verbs that can be converted into noun groups (see the table above for some suggestions).
- **Rewrite passages with noun groups** instead of verb-based clauses.
- You can make other additions as necessary – delete inessential words, replace general words with more specific ones, and so on. But you must try to preserve the intended meaning of the original writer.
- Remember: **there is no one right way to revise these passages.** You should strive to make the originals more concise and academic in style, but your revisions may – and should – vary from your classmates' versions.

Example 1

Original text:

When electrical engineers **invented** the computer chip, it revolutionized entire computer systems. – 2 clauses; 12 words.
Rewrite:

The **invention** of the computer chip revolutionized entire computer systems. – 1 clause; 10 words

Example 2

Original text:

Mechanical engineers **design** brakes that **will work** properly when the time comes. It is one of their most important tasks. If they were to **fail** at the wrong time, not only people in the vehicle, but even innocent bystanders may **die** as a result. – 6 clauses; 44 words

Rewrite:

One of mechanical engineers' most important tasks is the **design** of properly **working** breaks. Break **failure** at the wrong time can result in **deaths** of drivers, passengers, and innocent bystanders. – 2 clauses; 30 words.

1. In November 1971, the company named Intel introduced the first microprocessor, which was called Intel 4004. It contributed to the complex technology that has developed since then.

    _____
    _____
    _____
    _____
    _____

2. Every teen dreams of getting their driver's license and going anywhere they want to go. They see the driver's license as a way to discover new places and venture near or far. It encapsulates for them the very definition of freedom.

    _____
    _____
    _____
    _____
    _____

3. It's important to observe a child over a period of time and listen to what they are trying to say when they are using only one word. When we observe children, we notice how they build up their vocabulary and how they grow more independent in how they communicate. Once children acquire important distinctions between sounds in their native language, they can use these abilities to learn words. This shows that many connections are formed just by listening to the native language.

    _____
    _____
    _____
    _____
    _____
    _____

4. Hospitality Management is an industry that is growing faster than any other industry in the world. More and more people are majoring in Hospitality Management. There are many schools offering the Hospitality Management major and allowing people to learn about the hospitality industry. This major provides

many resources that allow students to get stable jobs after they graduate from college.

_____

_____

_____

_____

_____

_____

5. Many children in America live in poverty. Unfortunately, the majority of impoverished children remain poor. They often face many challenges in obtaining basic necessities such as food, water, shelter, and sanitation. Consequently, children of low-income families are affected the most. Poverty has been a major concern in the United States for many years.

_____

_____

_____

_____

_____

_____

PRACTICE 4.2-F

 ## Directions: Applying Your Knowledge to Self-Editing

Now it is time to apply the revision skills you've gained in this section to your own writing. Select a section of a paper you wrote or are currently writing for any class – preferably something in your major. The passage should be about 300 words long or more. Identify areas where you can revise the text to create more concise and informative noun groups by:

*   Converting verb-based clauses into noun groups
*   Making noun groups more specific by adding modifiers to them: adjectives, other nouns, or phrases beginning with prepositions.

4.3 HOW CAN I USE NOUN GROUPS TO MAKE GENERALIZATIONS?

After you work through this section of the chapter, you will be well on the way to say confidently:

🎯 I can distinguish between specific and generic references.

🎯 I can use generic references accurately to make claims, draw conclusions, provide definitions, and state facts.

PRACTICE 4.3-A

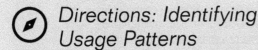

Directions: Identifying Usage Patterns

This exercise will help you explore two types of references writers use in their texts:

A. References to individually identifiable things, whether they are known to both the reader and the writer or only to the writer

B. References to one or many non-specific things that are representatives of a class or category

- Read through the text carefully and examine each underlined noun group.

- Ask yourself: does this group refer to some particular thing you can identify or just any non-specific thing that belongs to a group of things?

- Mark the noun groups as follows:

    - Ind – individual specific thing or person identifiable in the text

    - Gen – one non-specific thing or several non-specific things of many similar ones

- Discuss your choices with your group. Explain the reasoning behind your decisions to your groupmates.

From: Rogers, A. (2021). *How Pixar uses hyper-colors to hack your brain*. Wired. www.wired.com/story/how-pixar-uses-hyper-colors-to -hack-your-brain/#intcid=_wired-category-right-rail_eaf451a6-570a -4c1e-b34e-103ba3605d88_popular4-1.

Text	Type of Reference
(1) <u>The scene</u> wasn't working. It was a moment from (2) <u>the Pixar film *Coco*</u>, still in (3) <u>production</u> at the time— (4) <u>the part</u> when <u>the family of Miguel</u>, (5) <u>the main character</u>, finds out he's been hiding (6) <u>a guitar</u>. It takes place at (7) <u>twilight</u> or just after, (8) <u>a pink-and-purple-tinged time of day</u> everywhere, but even more so in fictional Pixarian Mexico. And Danielle Feinberg, (8) <u>the photography director in charge of lighting the movie</u>, didn't like it. She pressed Pause with a frown.	(1) – Ind (2) – Ind (3) – Gen
Lighting (9) <u>a computer-rendered Pixar movie</u> isn't like lighting (10) <u>a film with real actors and real sets</u>. (11) <u>The software Pixar uses</u> creates (12) <u>virtual sets</u> and (13) <u>virtual illumination</u>, just 1s and 0s, constrained only by the physics they're programmed with. Lights, pixels, action. (14) <u>Real-world cameras and lenses</u> have chromatic aberration, sensitivities or insensitivities to specific wavelengths of light, and ultimately limits to (15) <u>the colors they can sense and convey</u>—their gamut. But at Pixar (16) <u>the virtual cameras</u> can see an infinitude of light and color. The only real limit is (17) <u>the screen that will display the final product</u>. And it probably won't surprise you to hear that (18) <u>the Pixarians</u> are pushing those limits too.	

SUMMARY: GENERIC AND INDIVIDUAL REFERENCES

When a noun group refers to a member or members of a category rather than identifiable individual things, people, or ideas, the reference is called generic. A generic reference means "any one of X, not important which one" or "all of X(s)." The opposite of a generic reference is the specific or individual reference. Individual reference means "the X we both know about" or "an X/some Xs the writer knows about, but the reader doesn't yet."

Generic Reference	Individual Reference
Much like **a young writer** with **a pencil** or **a keyboard**, **young artists** use **cameras** to create **visual communications**.	Today, we will meet **a young writer** who can create vivid images through words and **a young artist** who uses **her camera** to bring still images to life.
The flow of water in **irrigation canals** must always be strictly controlled. Well-designed canal structures help achieve correct amounts of water delivered to different branches.	**Irrigation canals** in the area were damaged by the ashfall, which prevented the flow of water to the valley. Various illnesses were caused by the contaminated water obtained from **the irrigation canals**.
Shoulder dislocations are the most common dislocation injuries in **the human skeleton**.	**A human skeleton** presumed to be about 9,000 years old was unearthed in Wales.
Water pollution poses serious concerns about human health.	In order to reduce **the water pollution** in the region, the agency instituted stricter controls on the discharge of industrial byproducts near aquafers.

PRACTICE 4.3-B

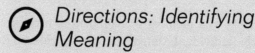

Directions: Identifying Meaning

In this exercise, you will explore the kinds of actions writers perform in their texts by using generic references.

- Read the passages below.
- Examine the underlined generic references in each.
- Decide what the writer is trying to do in each passage where he or she is using generic references:
    - A – Describe a common situation or process
    - B – Make a claim or state an opinion
    - C – Draw a conclusion from data or observations
    - D – Outline consequences or implications of actions
    - E – Provide a definition
- Discuss your choices with your group. **Each passage and sentence may do more than one clear-cut job in the text, so your choices may vary.**

Passages	Possible Decisions
<u>Improved health</u>, <u>wellbeing</u> and <u>quality of life</u> are associated with <u>older adults</u> living well at home. Enabling <u>older adults</u> to remain at home requires <u>organizations</u> to consider different workforce models to support these initiatives. <u>Volunteers</u> are often used by <u>organizations</u> providing such services. However, given the changing nature of the volunteer industry, <u>volunteer recruitment</u> and <u>retention practices</u> must be better understood. This study sought to understand individuals' motivations to volunteer in aged care home support.[10]	A – Describe a common situation or process B – Make a claim
Homeostasis in a general sense refers to <u>stability</u>, <u>balance</u> or <u>equilibrium</u>. It is <u>the body's</u> attempt to maintain <u>a constant internal environment</u>. Maintaining <u>a stable internal environment</u> requires constant monitoring and adjustments as <u>conditions</u> change. This adjusting of physiological systems within the body is called <u>homeostatic regulation</u>.[11]	

(Continued)

Passages	Possible Decisions
The results of the survey indicate <u>**that female managers**</u> report work to family conflict at levels higher than <u>**male managers**</u>, <u>**female non-managers**</u>, and <u>**male non- managers**</u>, thus providing support for our hypothesis. However, the effect sizes are smaller than we anticipated, suggesting that the levels of work-family conflict reported by <u>**female managers**</u> is unexpectedly similar to the levels of work to family conflict reported by <u>**male managers**</u>. <u>**A managerial main effect**</u> for the variable of work to family conflict further indicates that <u>**managerial status**</u> is <u>**an important predictor**</u> of work to family conflict.	
<u>**A career in Hospitality Management**</u> presents <u>**opportunities**</u> for <u>**graduates**</u> in a thriving, well-paying industry. The main responsibility of <u>**hospitality managers**</u> is to run day-to-day operations in <u>**hotels, resorts, restaurants, casinos, and travel businesses**</u>. <u>**An average day**</u> for such <u>**a manager**</u> includes supervising <u>**personnel**</u>, arranging for proper maintenance of the facilities, managing <u>**budgets**</u>, and ensuring <u>**customer satisfaction**</u>. In order to prepare industry leaders, <u>**hospitality management programs**</u> must provide students with a strong core of <u>courses in accounting, human resources, economics, and marketing</u>.	

SUMMARY: USES OF GENERIC REFERENCES IN ACADEMIC AND WORKPLACE WRITING

Meaning	Examples
To make a claim or state an opinion:	• Much like <u>a young writer</u> with <u>a pencil</u> or <u>a keyboard</u>, <u>young artists</u> use <u>cameras</u> to create <u>visual communications</u>. • There is <u>a belief</u> that <u>future-oriented planning</u> will lead to <u>more sustainable urban architecture</u>.
To draw a conclusion:	• We conclude that <u>expert testimony</u> describing the effects of trauma substantially assists <u>juries</u> in deciding on the verdict.
Outline implications of research or experiment:	• The experiment demonstrates that <u>simulations</u> may not be as successful in the industry as they have been in <u>laboratory settings</u>.
Describe a common process or situation:	• <u>**Shoulder dislocations**</u> are the most common <u>**dislocation injuries**</u> in <u>**the human skeleton**</u>. • As <u>additional data sets</u> are added to the calculations, the average values may change.

PRACTICE 4.3-C

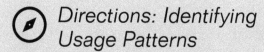

Directions: Identifying Usage Patterns

This exercise will draw your attention to the forms generic references can take.

• Read the sentences below and examine the underlined generic reference noun groups in them.
• Sort the noun groups by the kind of determiner that comes in front of them (*a*, *the*, or nothing Ø). Use the table under the text.
• What patterns do you observe? Discuss them with a classmate or a group.

1. The study suggests that **general word knowledge**, **morphological awareness**, and **exposure to print** are key factors in **a student's** ability to spell new words.
2. Your modem light may be blinking because **an automated process** is downloading **software updates** or performing **other housekeeping tasks**.
3. Despite its name, **the white rhino** is, in fact, dark grey. There are two genetically different subspecies of **the white rhino**: Northern and Southern. **The Northern white** rhino is on the brink of extinction.
4. **Pulmonary embolism** is **a life-threatening condition** in which **blood clots** travel from **deep veins** to **the lungs**, creating **blockages**, **impaired breathing**, and potentially even **death**.
5. **The printing press** was an incredible disrupting technology that altered how **humans** communicate, learn, and work, and even pray.
6. In the 1950s, a British physician, Dr. Simeons, discovered that the HCG hormone reacted positively with **the human body**, promoting **fat loss**. **Numerous later studies**, however, showed no relationship between HCG and **weight loss** or **appetite reduction**.

A/An + Noun	The + Noun	Ø + Noun
A student's (ability)	*The white rhino*	*General word knowledge*

Summarize the patterns in the use of *a/an, the,* and Ø with generic noun references:

- *A/an* is used with

  _____
  _____
  _____

- *The* is used with

  _____
  _____
  _____

- Ø is used with

  _____
  _____
  _____

SUMMARY: SINGULAR OR PLURAL?

Frequency	Usage	Examples
Most frequent	Use plural nouns to make statements about classes or categories of things	• _Non-traditional students_ are _adults_ who return to or begin attending college after a significant break from formal schooling. • _Electrons_ do not exist in a free state under _ambient environmental conditions_.
Less frequent	Use _the_ + singular noun to introduce conceptual representations or species	• Experts on endangered animals will meet to discuss the future of _the African elephant_. • Big companies like Samsung and LG pour millions of dollars into research that contributes to the evolution of _the smart phone_.
Least frequent	Use _a_ + singular noun to emphasize one random representative of a class or category	• Ten percent of adults prefer to engage in social media by using _a tablet_. • The cultural context in which _a child_ is raised can provide significant insights into the development of specific cognitive processes.

PRACTICE 4.3-D

 ## Directions: Editing

In this exercise, you will be applying the skills in making accurate and clear generic references.

* The passage below is an excerpt from a student essay. Read through it carefully to get the author's general idea.
* There are multiple problems with generic references in this passage. In the first sentence, they have been identified and corrected as an example. In the second sentence, they've been identified but not corrected. Please correct them. From the third sentence on, you will be identifying and correcting these problems on your own.
* Keep in mind that there may be several stylistic choices for correction, not just one. You need to choose the correction you

find the most appropriate and think about the reasoning for your choice.

- Once you've completed your editing, discuss your choices with a classmate. What are the reasons for the choices you made? Are there meaning or stylistic differences between different choices?

Computer *The computer* is one of the greatest inventions that impact our lives. It is very common for **the household** to own at least one computer or more. The software and applications created because of computer are incorporated in our lives in many ways. Around the 1990s, some of the computer science programmers created huge database for a network of networks, something we called "Internet," and this was soon followed by several other creations: chat rooms, blogs, and games. These online creations have quite an impact on social communications of mankind; furthermore, it changed the definition of our society.

The two main creations that internet has led to are online chat rooms and blogs. Chat room is defined as a branch of a computer network in which participants can engage in real-time discussions with one another. Such convenient electronic communications can have many benefits to it. Instead of phoning overseas, now one can talk with his relatives abroad through the use of internet and its software, such as messengers. Not only can one talk, but also seeing the other person has also become a possibility. Anyone can just stay home and conduct a video call on online messengers and experience an almost-the-same face-to-face situation.

4.4 HOW CAN I USE PRONOUNS FOR CLEAR AND FLUENT WRITING?

Pronouns are words that replace noun groups in a text. Using pronouns allows us to avoid repeating the same noun group over and over and, thus, make our writing smoother. Consider the following short passage from a scholarly article on carbon-monoxide poisoning[12]:

> *The authors* compared CO emission data with cases of CO poisoning. **They** concluded that there was a strong association between the reduction in vehicle exhaust CO emissions and the decreasing numbers of CO poisoning cases from 1985. **This** is likely to be a result of the introduction of catalytic converters in 1975.

There are two pronouns in this passage: **they** and **this**. The word **they** seems to clearly refer back to the noun group *the authors* in the previous sentence: as readers, we understand that **they** are the authors – i.e., the people who compared CO emission data with the cases of CO poisoning.

But what does the word **this** refer to? What is likely a result of the introduction of catalytic converters? The reduction in CO emissions? The decreasing number of CO poisoning cases? The observation that the authors make about the association between the two? Understanding what the word **this** means in this passage requires a bit of tricky interpretation because there is no single noun group that it indicates. Yet, we can still interpret its meaning. Most likely, the word **this** refers to a chain of events: (1) introduction of catalytic converters → (2) reduction in CO emissions → (3) reduction in the cases of CO poisoning.

However, the less the writer makes the reader work and backtrack the meaning in order to understand what noun groups or concepts pronouns refer to in the writer's text, the smoother and easier to read the text becomes. In this section, you will learn some skills that will help you make your reader's job in interpreting your pronominal references easier and, as a result, will help you become a more fluent writer.

After you work through this section of the chapter, you will be well on the way to say confidently:

- ◎ I know how to identify pronouns in a text.

- ◎ I know how to find which noun group each pronoun refers to.

- ◎ I know how to use pronouns clearly to refer to previously mentioned things.

- ◎ I know how to use phrases of the structure "this + noun" to reduce repetition and smooth the flow of my writing.

PRACTICE 4.4-A

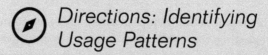 Directions: Identifying Usage Patterns

Your main objective in completing this exercise is to gain explicit awareness in how pronouns work to smooth out the flow of texts and refer to things already mentioned in a concise and clear way.

The passages below are excerpts from several public domain resources on nature conservation. The pronouns in them have been highlighted in bold-faced font.

- Read each passage carefully.
- **Draw a line** from the pronoun to the noun group it refers to. **Highlight** the noun group.
- **Mark** the pronoun-referent pairing in the column next to the passage.
- If it is not possible to easily identify a single noun group that the pronoun refers to, mark the pronoun-referent paring by summarizing the "referent" idea in your own words.
- The first two pronoun-referent pairings have been done as an example for you.
- After you complete the task, **discuss** the questions with a partner or a group and **summarize** your findings.

Excerpt 1

From: *The conservation movement at a crossroads: The Hetch Hetchy controversy*. Library of Congress Classroom Materials. www.loc.gov /classroom-materials/conservation-movement-at-a-crossroads-the -hetch-hetchy-controversy/

Text	Pronoun-Referent Pairing
Americans have a long history of advocating for the preservation of natural resources. Between 1850 and 1920 [naturalists, politicians, authors and artists] identified [numerous features of the natural and human landscape of America] which they believed worthy of preservation. They explained and justified their positions in lectures, articles, essays, books, and at congressional hearings. Out of this process, **they** formulated views on the nature of conservation itself and why governmental agencies and private individuals should conserve. **Their** ideas are as varied as the resources **which** **they** believe should be conserved.	*Which → "numerous features of the natural and human landscape of America"* *They → "naturalists, politicians, authors, and artists"*

Excerpt 2

From: Catalan, J., Ninot, J. M., & Mercè Aniz, M. (2017). *High mountain conservation in a changing world.* Advances in Global Change Research, 62. Apple Books. https://doi.org/10.1007/978 -3-319-55982-7_1. Retrieved from the Library of Congress Online. Digital ID: https://hdl.loc.gov/loc.gdc/gdcebookspublic.2019752759. Open book. Licensed under Creative Commons Attribution 4.0 International CC BY 4.0.

Text	Pronoun-Referent Pairing
The high mountains have retained a noticeable degree of wilderness even in the most populated regions of the planet. **This** is the reason why many nature reserves have been established in these landscapes. Currently, climate change and long-range transport of contaminants are affecting those protected areas, and thus conservation priorities may be challenged by these new pressures. In fact, many high mountains hold a legacy of on-site past human activities (e.g., pasturing, forestry, mining), **which** in some areas may partially persist, even increase, whereas in others are substituted by new uses (e.g., tourism, mountain sport).	

Excerpt 3

From: Huntley, B. J., Russo, V., Lages, F., & Ferrand, N. (2019). *Biodiversity in Angola.* Apple Books. https://doi.org/10.1007/978-3 -030-03083-4_1. Retrieved from the Library of Congress Online. Digital ID: https://hdl.loc.gov/loc.gdc/gdcebookspublic.2019758650. Open Book. Licensed under Creative Commons 4.0 International CC BY 4.0.

Text	Pronoun-Referent Pairing
Angola is a large country, and as emphasized throughout this volume, **it** has a rich diversity of landscapes, seascapes and associated biomes and ecoregions. The history of biodiversity research in Angola stretches over 200 years. The spatial, temporal and taxonomic scales embraced in this book results in **it** being structured in five parts. Part I, Chap. 1 (Huntley and Ferrand this chapter) provides an introduction to the book and its content.	

Discussion Questions

- Where is the referent of the pronoun usually located in the text: before the pronoun or after it?
- How far from the pronoun is the referent usually located (same sentence, one sentence apart, two sentences apart, etc.)?
- If the noun-group referent is several sentences away from the pronoun, how do we as readers know that this particular noun group is really what the pronoun refers to?

Summarize Your Findings

- Write a short paragraph (three to four sentences) reflecting on what you've learned about pronouns from this practice and the discussion with classmates.

PRACTICE 4.4-B

 Directions: Identifying Problems with Unclear Pronoun Referents

In this exercise, you will examine passages written by students. These passages contain some problematic uses of pronouns. It is not always clear what the pronouns refer to. In each passage, the problematic pronoun has been highlighted.

- Read each passage carefully.
- Think about which noun group or concept the pronoun can possibly refer to.
- Discuss with a partner how easy or difficult it is to interpret the pronoun's meaning and referent.
- After this discussion, formulate a suggestion for future writers (and yourself) on how to avoid similar problems with pronoun use in their own (and your) texts.

Example

Excerpt:

There are all many kinds of pollutants in the world. One is air, and the other one is water. Both forms of pollution construct dangerous environments for humans and animals, whether **they** are on land or sea. Both forms of pollution can kill anyone from a baby who is only one month old or an adult who is about one hundred years old because those pollutants can cause problems internally to externally.

Possible Pronoun Referents:

The referent of the pronoun "they" is unclear. It could be referring to

• *forms of pollution that exist on land or in the sea,*
• *the dangerous environments that are created on land or in the sea,*
• *or animals (and humans) who could be living on land and sea.*

Suggestions for Future Writers:

(1) *Replace an unclear pronoun with a noun group:*
    *Both forms of pollution construct dangerous environments for humans and animals, whether **these environments** are on land or in the sea. (they = the environments)*
(2) *Use verbs or adjectives that can apply only to one of several possible referents:*
    *Both forms of pollution construct dangerous environments for humans and animals, whether they **live** on land or in the sea. (live they = animals (and humans))*
(3) *Move the pronoun closer to its referent*
    *Both forms of pollution, whether **they** are on land or on the sea, construct dangerous environments for humans and animals. (they = forms of pollution)*

Excerpt 1

In Litke's (2007) article, **he** identifies two primary reasons for engine inefficiency: the age of the engine and incomplete fuel ignition. If the fuel does not ignite completely in the combustion chamber due to the velocity of the airflow, unburned particles may be carried out and exhausted into the environment.

Possible Pronoun Referents

_____
_____
_____

Suggestions for Future Writers

_____
_____
_____
_____
_____
_____
_____

Excerpt 2

Climate change is becoming a global concern. Aircraft are the only source of high-altitude emissions, **which** amplifies the severity of the situation. Aerospace engineers must prioritize improving developing new aircraft propulsion technologies to reduce our carbon footprint.

Possible Pronoun Referents

_____
_____
_____

Suggestions for Future Writers

_____
_____
_____
_____
_____
_____
_____

Excerpt 3

According to Maslow's hierarchy of needs, belonging and love needs as well as safety needs are essential for our everyday life. Without feeling safe and secure or not feeling the affection and love of others will make us feel very unsafe and empty. Many teenagers seek for belonging and love but forget about being safe and expose themselves to being abused. Due to **this**, one out of three teens is abused in a relationship, and we, as a community should do something to help prevent **this**.

Possible Pronoun Referents

_____

_____

_____

Suggestions for Future Writers

_____

_____

_____

_____

_____

_____

_____

Excerpt 4

Since advanced education has become more prevalent and widely accessible, modern students who are assured a place at an institution of higher learning have begun to turn their sights to their post-high school lives. The issue of employability after college is a great concern for many. There are many interesting majors in college but not all of them are practical or have the potential of a well-paying job. **They** worry about whether **they** can find a job after graduation.

Possible Pronoun Referents

_____

_____

_____

Suggestions for Future Writers

_____

_____

_____

_____

_____

_____

_____

Excerpt 5

The first successful case of blood transfusion took place in England in the 17th century. But blood was not transfused from human to human yet. Instead, a doctor named Richard Lower transferred blood to a dog from other dogs and kept <u>it</u> alive. Human-to-human transfusions started to be used in the 19th century to treat postpartum bleeding and blood disorders like hemophilia. Since World Word II, <u>it</u> has been a common procedure to save lives.

Possible Pronoun Referents

_____

_____

_____

Suggestions for Future Writers

_____

_____

_____

_____

_____

_____

_____

PRACTICE 4.4-C

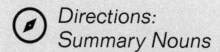

Directions: Summary Nouns

The purpose of this exercise is to help you identify summary nouns – nouns that help writers make pronouns such as *this*, *these*, and *such* less ambiguous when they refer to ideas and concepts rather than specific noun groups. In the table below, you will find several passages from published texts.

- Read each passage in the left-hand column carefully. A combination of a pronoun and a summary noun – *this* + *noun* – has been underlined in it.
- Determine which idea or concept this combination refers to.
- Write the concept in the right-hand column in your own words.
- The first one has been done for you as an example.

Text	Concept
Americans have a long history of advocating for the preservation of natural resources. Between 1850 and 1920 naturalists, politicians, authors and artists identified numerous features of the natural and human landscape of America which they believed worthy of preservation. They explained and justified their positions in lectures, articles, essays, books, and at congressional hearings. Out of **this process**, they formulated views on the nature of conservation itself and why governmental agencies and private individuals should conserve. Their ideas are as varied as the resources which they believe should be conserved[13].	*this process = identifying and advocating for parts of the United States' landscape that should be protected*
The debate over damming the Hetch Hetchy Valley in Yosemite National Park marked a crossroads in the American conservation movement. Until **this debate**, conservationists seemed fairly united in their aims. San Francisco's need for a reliable water supply, along with a new political dynamic at the federal level, created a division between those committed to preserving the wilderness and those more interested in efficient management of its use. While **this confrontation** happened nearly one hundred years ago, it contains many of the same arguments which are used today whenever preservationists and conservationists mobilize.[13]	
The high mountains have retained a noticeable degree of wilderness even in the most populated regions of the planet. This is the reason why many nature reserves have been established in **these landscapes**. Currently, climate change and long-range transport of contaminants are affecting **those protected areas**, and thus conservation priorities may be challenged by these new pressures. In fact, many high mountains hold a legacy of on-site past human activities (e.g., pasturing, forestry, mining), which in some areas may partially persist, even increase, whereas in others are substituted by new uses (e.g., tourism, mountain sport).[14]	
Angola possesses an unusually rich diversity of ecosystems and species, but **this natural wealth** is poorly documented when compared with other countries in the region. Both colonial history and extended wars challenged progress in biodiversity research and conservation, but since peace was achieved in 2002 a rapidly increasing level of collaboration between Angolan and visiting scientists and institutions has seen a blossoming of biodiversity research.[15]	

PRACTICE 4.4-D

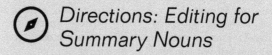

Directions: Editing for Summary Nouns

In this exercise, your goal is to edit passages written by students like you to clarify the meaning of pronouns.

- In each passage, the pronouns *this* or *these* are highlighted. They refer to an idea, noun group, or concept expressed in the text just before them, but their meaning is, nevertheless, vague.
- **Clarify** this meaning by **inserting an appropriate summary noun** after each highlighted pronoun.
- You can choose from the summary nouns listed above the passages, but you are encouraged to choose your own.
- Keep in mind that it may be advantageous sometimes to change the pronoun *this* for *these* and vice versa to include the best summary noun for the context. Make sure to adjust the verbs for subject-verb agreement if you change singular pronouns and summary nouns to plural ones and the other way around.

Example

Original passage:

Teenagers want to be popular for one reason, and that is to have more confidence in their lives. **This** is one of the most important factors we take into consideration with our products because it is very important for successful sales.

Revision:

Teenagers want to be popular for one reason, and that is to have more confidence in their lives. ***This desire*** is one of the most important factors we take into consideration with our products because it is very important for successful sales.

Sample Summary Nouns

fashion	monument	thinking	hotel	sculpture
actions	style	step	schools	courses
building	quote	trend	line of thought	clothes
claim	lack of classes	words	engagement	piece of art
programs	movement	shortage	historical structure	view

1. Every time adults, especially parents, see the hip-hop fashion among teenagers, they think of them as lazy, irresponsible slackers. **This** occurs because hip-hop style has become a symbol for criminals and gangsters. Although such clothing is commonly worn by such people, **this** was intended for teenagers to become more popular and increase their self-esteem.

___

2. Created 135 years ago, the Mission Inn Hotel has been part of many historical events in Riverside. **This** contains much of the history of the city and the county. Although there are many famous hotels all over the world, the Mission Inn deserves more than just a mere recognition.

___

3. South of the park center, giant figures posed as if battling each other on top of elephants are located. Two elephants with two men battle each other, and some people on the ground fight each other as well. **This** is dedicated to the most important battle during the Independence War.

___

4. One of the main obstacles for timely graduation is the ratio of available classes to the number of students who need to take them. There are a lot more students than there are classes for them. **This** becomes a concern for **those** who want to graduate as quickly as possible.

___

5. Animal testing of cosmetics has painfully injured and wasted millions of animal lives. We, as the primary consumers of the tested products, should advocate for the ban on animal testing when other, less cruel methods of checking cosmetics for safety are available. **This** is important for creating a fairer and more ethical world.

___

6. The first step in becoming a commercial pilot is to find a local flight school that you can easily attend. There are a lot of flight schools out there that you can search for, but it is recommended to apply for a Federal Aviation Administration (FAA) approved schools for building your flight hours. There are also universities and colleges with flight training programs approved by FAA, and **these** will ultimately help you finish your classes as fast as possible and start to train you on how to fly.

___

7. In his essay, "I Just Wanna be Average", Mike Rose states, "Students will float to the mark you set." **This** means that students who lack challenges and motivation provided by their teachers would always believe that they can only meet the lower standards of education and would only do the bare minimum that is set for them.

PRACTICE 4.4-E

 Directions: Applying your Knowledge to Self-Editing

Now, it is your turn. Select a piece of your own writing approximately 300–500 words long. It can be an excerpt from an essay, a lab report, a case study, or a research paper – and edit it for the strength of your claims.

- Read your work one time through to remind yourself of your argument and supporting points.
- Read your work again, this time highlighting all pronouns, focusing specifically on the pronouns *this, that, these, those,* or *such.*
- Examine the passages before and immediately after these pronouns:

  - Is there a summary noun after each pronoun?
  - If not, is the meaning of the pronoun absolutely clear without such a noun? Will the meaning become clearer if a summary noun is added?
  - Add the appropriate summary noun.
  - If there is a summary noun after the pronoun, what does it refer to in your text? Is this an appropriate summary noun? If necessary, revise the summary noun.

NOTES

1 From: Ahmadi, S., Marszalek, J, Gutierrez, G.L., & Uchida, M. C. (2020). Sitting volleyball players: Differences in physical and psychological characteristics between national and league teams. *Kinesiology, 52*(2), 169–177.

2 Minneapolis Star Tribune. (2019, January 27). In the first of four Minneapolis shows, Neil Young becomes mellow, reflective 'Old Man'. www.startribune .com/in-the-first-of-four-minneapolis-shows-neil-young-becomes-mellow -reflective-old-man/504933701/

3 Adapted from: Gibbens, S. (June 5, 2019). You eat thousands of bits of plastic every year. *National Geographic.* www.nationalgeographic.com/ environment/article/you-eat-thousands-of-bits-of-plastic-every-year

4 Shpigel, B., Cacciola, S., & Schonbrun, Z. (2019, January 20). In the din of the Dome, the Rams beat the Saints in overtime. *The New York Times.* www.nytimes.com/2019/01/20/sports/football/nfl-playoffs-live-nfc -championship-rams-vs-saints.html.

5 Daily Kos Community. www.dailykos.com/stories/2012/05/13/1091415/ -OMG-Republican-Heads-Are-Going-To-Explode.

6 Evans, L. (2019, August 14). Researchers find that arctic ice is filled with microplastics. *Jezebel.* https://jezebel.com/researchers-find-that-arctic-ice -is-filled-with-micropl-1837260533.

7 Author bio. *The Dallas Morning News.* www.dallasnews.com/news/politics /2019/09/10/elizabeth-warren-assails-corruption-promises-change-as -democrats-swarm-to-texas/.

8 Science Daily (2019, September 5). Coffee may protect against gallstones. www.sciencedaily.com/releases/2019/09/190905080059.htm

9 Sources for sentences in the table:
   1. Shen, Y., Karimi, K., Law, S., & Zhong, C. (2019). Physical co-presence intensity: Measuring dynamic face-to-face interaction potential in public space using social media check-in records. *PLoS ONE, 14*(2): e0212004. https://doi.org/10.1371/journal.pone.0212004
   2. Konzen, K. N., Gerber, D. A., Morawska, E., Pozzetta, G. E., & Vecoli, R. J. (1992). The invention of ethnicity: A perspective from the U.S.A. *Journal of American Ethnic History, 12*(1), 3–41.
   3. Dolly, J. P. (1993). The impact of juku on Japanese students. *Journal of Instructional Psychology, 20*(4), 277–285.
   4. Kim, H. (2019, February 1). Vehicle detection and speed estimation for automated traffic surveillance systems at nighttime. *Tehniki Vjestnic – Technical Gazette, 26*(1), 87–94.

10 Same, A., McBride, H., Liddelow, C., Mullan, B., & Harris, C. (2020). Motivations for volunteering time with older adults: A qualitative study. *PLoS ONE, 15*(5), e0232718. https://doi.org/10.1371/journal.pone.0232718 Licensed under Creative Commons License CC-BY.

11 Wikibooks (2013). Human physiology. Licensed under Creative Commons Attribution-Share Alike 3.0 Unported License.

12 Simonsen, C., Thornsteinsson, K., Mortensen, K. R., Torp-Pedersen, C., Kjærgaard, B., & Andreasen, J. J. (2019). Carbon monoxide poisoning in Denmark with focus on mortality and factors contributing to mortality. *PLoS ONE, 14*(1), e0210767. https://doi.org/10.1371/journal.pone.0210767

13 *The conservation movement at a crossroads: The Hetch Hetchy controversy.* Library of Congress Classroom Materials. www.loc.gov/classroom-materials /conservation-movement-at-a-crossroads-the-hetch-hetchy-controversy/ Public domain.

14 Catalan, J., Ninot, J. M., & Mercè Aniz, M. (2017). *High mountain conservation in a changing world.* Advances in Global Change Research, 62. Apple Books. https://doi.org/10.1007/978-3-319-55982-7_1. Retrieved from the Library of Congress Online. Digital ID: https://hdl.loc.gov/loc.gdc/gdcebookspublic .2019752759. Open book. Licensed under Creative Commons Attribution 4.0 International CC BY 4.0.

15 Huntley, B. J., Russo, V., Lages, F., & Ferrand, N. (2019). *Biodiversity of Angola.* https://doi.org/10.1007/978-3-030-03083-4. Retrieved from the Library of Congress Online. Digital ID: https://hdl.loc.gov/loc.gdc/gdcebookspublic .2019758650 Licensed under Creative Commons 4.0 International CC BY 4.0.

▣ 5

Using Grammatical Tools for Clarity

What comes to your mind when you hear the word *elegant*?

In ordinary conversation, we often use the word to describe something stylish, classy, fashionable, beautiful, and maybe even dainty. But think about how you might use the word in your field of study. If you are a programmer or a computer scientist, what does an *elegant code* mean to you? If you are a student of engineering or architecture, what kind of image do you have in mind when you think of an *elegant design*? If your interest and future career lie in mathematics or sciences, what, to you, constitutes an *elegant formula*, an *elegant graph*, or an *elegant solution* to a problem?

Stop reading here for a minute and jot down your ideas on a piece of paper or a note app.

Now look at your notes. In thinking about something from your field that can be described as *elegant*, you probably thought that it is generally functional and simple, clear, coherent, and powerful.

When something is simple, it has only the necessary elements or information; it is not cluttered by anything that doesn't contribute to its meaning or function.

When something is clear, it is easy to follow and understand.

When something is coherent, it is logical, well-organized, and consistent. It flows effortlessly for the reader or user. It does not cause confusion. In other words, it is user- (or reader-) friendly.

When something is powerful, it can do a lot of things or be used for multiple purposes. A powerful concept explains a lot of phenomena. A powerful solution provides answers to big problems or many problems at once. A powerful design communicates ideas effectively, invokes a strong response in the user, and leaves a lasting impression.

DOI: 10.4324/9781003159889-6

So far, you have learned a lot of ways to make your writing simple, clear, and coherent, from choosing the right verbs and their forms to building informative and concise noun groups, to varying your sentence structure and using effective punctuation. Knowing how to use these structures effectively helps you declutter your texts, make your ideas logical and easy to understand, and make an important impact on your readers.

This chapter will take you one step further: you will learn just a few more elements of style that go beyond particular parts of speech and cut across different types of sentences. When you use these elements, you will be able to lead your reader smoothly from one idea to another and eliminate certain stylistic stumbling blocks that may cause confusion. These elements are:

- Parallelism in sentence and paragraph organization
- Avoidance of misplaced (aka dangling) modifiers
- Choosing word forms appropriate for the context

This chapter consists of three sections, each of which will address one of these elements of style:

5.1   Parallel structure
5.2   Misplaced modifiers
5.3   Word forms and frequently confused words

5.1 HOW DO I PRESENT IDEAS IN A LIST OR SHOW IDEAS WITH EQUAL IMPORTANCE?

After you work through this section of the chapter, you will be well on the way to say confidently:

◎ I can identify patterns of words and word groups in a list.

◎ I can streamline my writing by using the same patterns of words and word groups to show that the ideas they represent are of equal importance.

PRACTICE 5.1-A

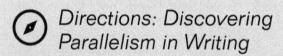

Directions: Discovering Parallelism in Writing

This exercise is designed to help you discover what parallelism in writing is and how it works. The excerpt below is from an undergraduate college textbook on business law.

- First, read through the text, focusing on its meaning and message. Do not worry about the grammar.
- Second, go back to the beginning of the text and read it again, this time focusing on the highlighted stretches. Each of these stretches is a list of things, actions, qualities, or phenomena.
- In each list, identify individual items.
- Then, determine the category of the items. How are the categories similar or different in each list?
- An example is provided for you below the text.

Text:

From: Valbrune, M., De Assis, R., Cardel, S., Taylor, T.C., Sappleton, N., Mitchell, C.M., & Mitchell-Phillips, K. (2019). *Business law essentials*. OpenStax, Rice University. Licensed under Creative License Attribution 4.0 International License (CC BY 4.0). Access for free at openstax.org.

The American legal system has its roots in the British legal system. It was developed with the purpose of **establishing standards for** acceptable conduct, prescribing punishment for violations as a deterrent, establishing systems for enforcement, and peacefully resolving disputes. The ultimate goal of the American legal system is promotion of the common good.

Establishing Standards

The American legal system was developed with the goal of establishing a set of standards that outline what is to be considered minimally acceptable behavior. Broadly speaking, federal laws are those that all United States citizens are expected to follow. **State and local laws may often be similar to federal laws**, but **they may also differ quite a bit**, and only govern the state's citizens.

Promoting Consistency

The American legal system follows the British Common Law system, which is designed to leverage past judicial reasoning, while also promoting fairness through consistency. Judges in the Common Law system help shape the law through **their rulings** and **interpretations**. This body of past decisions is known as case law. Judges use case law to inform their own rulings. Indeed, judges rely on precedent, i.e., previous court rulings on similar cases, for ruling on their own cases.

All U.S. states, except Louisiana, have enacted "reception statutes," stating that the judge-made common law of England is the law of the state to the extent that it does not conflict with the state's current laws.

However, the body of American law is now so robust that American cases rarely cite English materials, except for a British classic or a famous old case. Additionally, foreign law is not cited as binding precedent. Therefore, the current American practice of the common law tradition refers more to the process of judges looking to the precedent set jurisdictionally, and is substantially similar to American case law.

Maintaining Order

Congruent with the goal of establishing standards and promoting consistency, laws are also used **to promote, provide, and maintain order**.

Resolving Disputes

Conflicts are to be expected given people's varying **needs, desires, objectives, values systems, and perspectives**. The American legal system provides a formal means for resolving conflicts through the courts. In addition to **the federal court and individual state systems**, there are also several informal means for resolving disputes that are collectively called alternative dispute resolution (ADR). Examples of these are **mediation and arbitration**.

Protecting Liberties and Rights

The United States Constitution and state laws provide people with many **liberties** and **rights.** American laws operate with **the purpose** and **function of protecting these liberties and rights** from violations **by persons, companies, governments, or other entities**.

Based on the British legal system, the American legal system is divided into **a federal system** and **a state and local system**. The overall goal of both systems **is to provide order** and **a means of dispute settlement**, as well as **to protect citizens' rights**.

Clearly, the purposes of the American legal system are **broad** and **well-considered**.

Sentence	Items in a List	Conclusions about the Items
Example: *[The American legal system] was developed with the purpose of establishing standards for acceptable conduct, prescribing punishment for violations as a deterrent, establishing systems for enforcement, and peacefully resolving disputes.*	*Example:* • *Establishing standards for acceptable conduct* • *Prescribing punishment for violations as a deterrent* • *Establishing systems for enforcement* • *Peacefully resolving disputes*	*Example:* *All items in a list are -ing phrases; in them, the main word is an -ing verb; the verb sometimes has objects (e.g., establishing standards; prescribing punishment, etc.) and sometimes an adverb modifying it (e.g., peacefully resolving), but the verb itself, in the -ing form, is always the main word. The same structure is used for all items in a list.*

(Continued)

Sentence	Items in a List	Conclusions about the Items
(1) State and local laws may often be similar to federal laws, but they may also differ quite a bit.		
(2) Judges in the Common Law system help shape the law through their rulings and interpretations.		
(3) …laws are also used to promote, provide, and maintain order.		
(4) Conflicts are to be expected given people's varying needs, desires, objectives, values systems, and perspectives.		
(5) The United States Constitution and state laws provide people with many liberties and rights.		
(6) In addition to the federal court and individual state systems, there are also several informal means for resolving disputes that are collectively called alternative dispute resolution (ADR).		
(7) Examples of these are mediation and arbitration.		

(Continued)

Sentence	Items in a List	Conclusions about the Items
(8) American laws operate with the purpose and function of protecting these liberties and rights from violations by persons, companies, governments, or other entities.		
(9) ...the American legal system is divided into a federal system and a state and local system.		
(10) The overall goal of both systems is to provide order and a means of dispute settlement, as well as to protect citizens' rights.		
(11) Clearly, the purposes of the American legal system are broad and well-considered.		

SUMMARY: PARALLELISM WITHIN A SENTENCE

What

Definition	Types	Examples
Parallelism – aka parallel structure – is using the same word type, word-group type, or clause type for all items in a list. These types of structures can include but are not limited to the list to the right.	*Verb groups (here: present tense):*	Turbulence inside the cloud creates dense pockets that collapse to forge new stars. Those stars then <u>launch</u> powerful jets, <u>give off</u> radiation, <u>shed</u> stellar winds and <u>explode</u> in supernovas.[1]
	Verb groups (-ing forms):	<u>**Establishing**</u> **clear conduct rules and** <u>**providing**</u> **straightforward guidelines for workplace communication** can help companies avoid lawsuits.
	Nouns:	...the researchers measured greenhouse gases wafting off **dead** <u>**trees**</u> **and** <u>**soil**</u> in five ghost forests on the Albemarle-Pamlico Peninsula in North Carolina.[2]
	Adjectives:	...researchers think that heavy elements are more likely forged in collisions of two <u>**dense**</u>**,** <u>**dead**</u> stars called neutron stars, or in certain rare types of supernovas, such as those that form from fast-spinning stars.[3]
	Prepositional phrases:	...researchers think that heavy elements are more likely forged <u>**in**</u> **collisions of two dense, dead stars called neutron stars**, or <u>**in**</u> **certain rare types of supernovas**, such as those that form from fast-spinning stars.
	Clauses:	The group claims <u>**that**</u> **it supports only non-violent reform and** <u>**that**</u> **none of its members are connected to terrorist organizations.**

Why

Clarity	Without Parallelism	With Parallelism
Using parallel structure makes it easier for the reader to follow the writer's train of thought and argument.	*Choppy and hard to follow:* The World Bank is a UN organization <u>**financed**</u> **by contributions from developed countries and** <u>**is**</u> **in Washington, DC.** *Financed* – an -ed adjective/participle *Is* – present tense verb	*Smooth and easy to follow:* The World Bank is a UN organization <u>**financed**</u> **by contributions from developed countries and** <u>**headquartered**</u> **in Washington, DC.** *Financed* and *headquartered* – both -ed adjectives/participles

How to Edit	
Step	*Examples*
Step 1: *Identify the list or series:*	When we think of airplane safety, we have to take into consideration other factors that might influence the safety of the aircraft, for example **the pilot's training**, **what the weather is like**, **if there is a threat of terrorism**, and **the condition of the runway.**
Step 2: *Write the items in the list or series vertically AND/ OR underline the core word or word in each item:*	the pilot's <u>training</u> <u>what the weather is like</u> <u>if there is a threat of terrorism</u> the <u>**condition**</u> of the runway
Step 3: *Determine the type of the word, word group, or clause in the list or series:*	the pilot's <u>training</u> (noun group – what) <u>what the weather is like</u> (what-clause) <u>if there is a threat of terrorism</u> (if-clause) the <u>**condition**</u> of the runway (noun group – what)
Step 4: *Choose the type of word group or clause that you prefer and turn all the items into that form:*	All noun groups: When we think of airplane safety we have to take into consideration other factors that might influence the safety of the aircraft, for example **the pilot's training, the weather conditions, the potential threat of terrorism, and the condition of the runway.**

	OR All clauses: When we think of airplane safety we have to take into consideration other factors that might influence the safety of the aircraft, for example **whether the pilot has been trained properly, what the weather is like, if there is a threat of terrorism, and what the condition of the runways is like.**

Caveats: More Editing Tips	
Tips	*Examples*
Tip 1: You do not have to repeat short words like *to, has, will, for,* etc. if they appear at the beginning of each word group in a series, especially if this word group is relatively short:	This can lead **to delays in flights** and **(to) increases in the prices of airplane tickets.** `Optional`

Tip 2: If there are a lot of words in each list item, it is useful to keep the small words in the text to help the reader identify where each item ends and a new one begins:	To answer this question, we need **to examine the features of online learning sites providing practical exercises** and **to study the students' behaviors and feelings while they engage with these sites.**
Tip 3: It is okay to have different first function words (e.g., prepositions or helping verbs) in each item as long as these first words reflect closely related meanings:	Both of these problems could have been prevented if the companies acted **as soon as they received the notices about malfunctions** and **before any serious accident occurred.** (Both "as soon as" and "before" specify time).
Tip 4: All items on the list or in a series need to be equal in function <u>and</u> meaning, not only in form:	NOT OK: John was clearing snow **with a shovel** and **with a vengeance.** OK: John was clearing the snow **with a shovel** and **(with) a snowblower.** OK: John was clearing the snow **with a vengeance** and **(with) gusto.**

PRACTICE 5.1-B

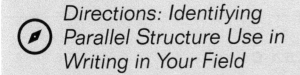

Directions: Identifying Parallel Structure Use in Writing in Your Field

The purpose of this practice is to identify common ways writers use parallel structure in your major, field of study, and/or work.

- Find a passage from a reading in your major or a publication related to your job. This can be a textbook from a major class, or a professional trade magazine or newsletter, or a research article. You may want to ask a professor in your major to point you to such a publication. Make sure that the passage is at least 200 words long.
- Underline all lists or series in this passage and identify all items in each list or series.
- Examine each item and analyze its structure.
- Use the questions below to identify and discuss patterns you notice.
- Summarize your findings below.

Discussion Questions

- How frequently are lists or series used in writing in your field?
- What types of structures commonly occur in these series or lists?
- What can you do in your own writing to imitate the style typical of your field?

Summarize Your Findings

- Write a short paragraph (three to four sentences) reflecting on what you've learned from analyzing a sample of writing in your major, field of study, or work and discussing the patterns with classmates.

_____

_____

_____

_____

_____

_____

_____

_____

PRACTICE 5.1-C

 Directions: Editing

In this exercise, you will practice detecting disruptions in parallelism and correcting them. The sentences and passages below come from typical student essays in a variety of classes.

- Read each passage carefully.
- Underline the elements that belong to a list or series.
- Identify the type of structure used for the elements.
- Select the structure you find most appropriate and correct the sentences.

1. The purpose of this paper is to consider the causes of the current CD sales decline and shows a possible marketing strategy for CDs.

    _____
    _____
    _____
    _____
    _____

2. High school is a place to discover what you are really interested in. Teens go through their phases. One day they want to be in a band; other days they aspire to be the president of the United States, and other days they are daydreaming of being in front of millions at Fenway Park. In my case, all my daydreams were full of golden statues, big screens, and being famous.

    _____
    _____
    _____
    _____
    _____

3. The way that a mechanical engineer would go about preventing something like this from happening is by trying to recreate the problem and what caused the accident and then identify the best possible solution for this problem.

    _____
    _____
    _____
    _____
    _____

4. A calf requires a lot of vegetation in order to get to up to the suitable weight, 500-600 pounds, to be put on the slaughter line or to be used for milk production. All of the vegetation it consumes is contaminated and retains it in its body, becoming contaminated.

    _____
    _____
    _____
    _____
    _____

5. A large number of students in high school and college suffer from sleep deprivation. Research, however, has found ways to prevent loss of sleep and improvement in academic performance if school started later in the day.

6. Landscape architects integrate their design skills in the development of neighborhoods, towns, cities, and larger commercial areas. Landscape architects are also included in the planning of highways and parkways to provide attractive views as well as creating efficient means of traffic circulation.

PRACTICE 5.1-D

 Directions: Discovering Textual Parallelism

Effective writing is parallel in many ways. Not only does parallelism help smooth out individual sentences, but it also works at the level of the whole text. In this exercise, you will explore how parallelism works beyond a single sentence.

- Return to the text in Practice 5.1-A in this chapter.
- Reread the text and take notes to observe the ideas below.

Observation 1: What are the purposes of the U.S. legal system as listed in the first paragraph?

_____

_____

_____

_____

Observation 2: Compare the order in which each purpose is introduced in the thesis and the order in which it is discussed in the text. What do you observe?

_____

_____

_____

_____

Observation 3: Examine each subheading. What is the grammatical form of each subheading?

_____

_____

_____

_____

Observation 4: Examine the structure of each paragraph discussing each individual purpose of the American legal system. Look at the topic sentences, the content, and the concluding sentences of each. What do you observe?

_____

_____

_____

_____

Observation 5: List all the resources the authors are using in this text to streamline the information and help the reader follow it easily.

_____

_____

_____

_____

SUMMARY: PARALLELISM IN ORGANIZING A TEXT

Strategy	Example	Explanation
Use the same order of the paragraphs or sections in the text in which you first announce them.	Order of topics in the thesis of the U.S. legal system text: 1. **Establishing standards** 2. Prescribing punishment 3. **Establishing enforcement** 4. **Resolving disputes** Order of paragraphs elaborating on the thesis: 1. **Establishing standards** 2. Promoting consistency 3. **Maintaining order (i.e., enforcement)** 4. **Resolving disputes** 5. Protecting rights and liberties	Observation: Although some topics in the thesis are missing from the text, and some text topics are missing from the thesis, the topics that are present in both are in the same order in both.
Use the same style or structure of subheadings throughout the text.	Subheadings in the U.S. legal system text: • Establish**ing** Standards • Promot**ing** Consistency • Maintain**ing** Order • Resolv**ing** Disputes • Protect**ing** Liberties and Rights	Observation: All subheadings are -ing word groups. It is not a mandatory format, but it is consistent among all the subheadings.
Use the same paragraph or subsection organization to describe and discuss similar concepts.	Topic sentences of the subsections in the U.S. legal system text: • The American legal system was developed with the goal of **establishing a set of standards** that outline what is to be considered minimally acceptable behavior. • The American legal system follows the British Common Law system, which is designed to leverage past judicial reasoning, while also **promoting fairness through consistency.** • Congruent with the goal of establishing standards and promoting consistency, laws are also used to promote, provide, and **maintain order.** • The American legal system provides a **formal means for resolving conflicts** through the courts. (Second sentence in the subsection.) • American laws operate with the purpose and function of **protecting these liberties and rights** from violations by persons, companies, governments, or other entities. (Second section in the subsection.)	Observation: All subsections contain a topic sentence at the beginning (first or second sentence) that repeats the words from the subheading of the section or uses close synonyms of these words. The rest of the subsection explains and elaborates on the topic sentence. No subsection is lacking a clear topic sentence or places this topic sentence at the end. The structure of each subsection is the same.

PRACTICE 5.1-E

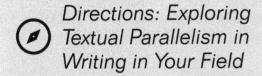 *Directions: Exploring Textual Parallelism in Writing in Your Field*

The purpose of this practice is to identify common ways writers use parallelism in the organization of texts in your major, field of study, and/or work.

- Find a passage from a reading in your major or a publication related to your job. This can be a textbook from a major class, or a professional trade magazine or newsletter, or a research article. You may want to ask a professor in your major to point you to such a publication. Make sure that the passage is at least two pages long.
- Examine the text carefully, looking for instances of text parallelism:
  - The order of topics, problems, or issues
  - The format of subheadings
  - A possible repetition of phrases
  - The organization of paragraphs or sections discussing each topic, problem, or issue
- Use the questions below to identify and discuss patterns you notice.
- Summarize your findings below.

Discussion Questions

- Is the passage easy to follow?
- Which resources that the author(s) used help you as a reader follow the progression of ideas in the text? Which ones make it more difficult?
- Are there any suggestions you could make to the author to improve the flow of the text through parallelism? If yes, what are they?

Summarize Your Findings

- Write a short paragraph (three to four sentences) reflecting on what you've learned from analyzing a sample of writing in your major, field of study, or work and discussing the patterns with classmates.

_____

_____

_____

_____

_____

_____

_____

_____

PRACTICE 5.1-F

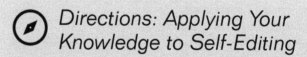 *Directions: Applying Your Knowledge to Self-Editing*

Now it is time to apply the revision skills you've gained in this section to your own writing. Select a section of a paper you wrote or are currently writing for any class – preferably something in your major. The passage should be about 300 words long or more. Read through the text carefully and identify the areas where its flow can be improved by increasing parallelism both at the sentence level and at the text level. Remember to complete each of the following:

- Streamline lists of ideas or points by using the same grammatical form for each idea/point.
- Match the order of ideas discussed in the text to the order in which they are introduced at the beginning.
- Use the same format or style for subheadings, if relevant.
- Reorganize individual paragraphs discussing each idea or point in a similar pattern to show their equal status.
- Revise your original text to improve the flow through parallelism.

5.2 HOW CAN I CLARIFY MY WRITING THROUGH THE PLACEMENT OF MODIFIERS?

After you work through this section of the chapter, you will be well on the way to say confidently:

 I can identify misplaced modifiers.

 I can revise my writing to remove ambiguity resulting from misplaced modifiers.

PRACTICE 5.2-A

> ### ◈ Directions: Identifying Misplaced Modifiers
>
> The aim of this practice is to help you identify misplaced modifiers in sentences, discuss why they are considered "misplaced," and discover how they affect the meaning of the sentences. All the sentences in this practice have been collected from the papers undergraduate students wrote for a variety of classes.
>
> * Read each sentence carefully.
> * Answer the question about the sentence.
> * The first sentence is done for you as an example.

1. **Sentence:** While passing through the valley of mountain streams, some of the maple leaves fall from the Japanese maple and float onto the cold water.

    Question: Who was passing through the valley of mountain streams? What does the reader need to know to figure this out?

    Sample Answer: *It sounds like some of the maple leaves were passing through the valley because they are the subject of the sentence. The sentence is about the maple leaves. But leaves do not pass through valleys. We can guess that it is the writer who was passing through the valley and observed how the leaves fall. The sentence is confusing and requires us to reread it to guess who was passing based on our understanding that people can pass through* *valleys and leaves can't, especially not when they are still on the trees.*

2. **Sentence:** When testing my first participant, the four-year-old used diminutive suffixes at the end of each word.
   Question: Who tested the writer's first participant? What does the reader need to know to figure this out?

   _____

   _____

   _____

   _____

   _____

   _____

3. **Sentence:** Divided into eighteen chapters, each chapter in *¡Claro que sí!* focuses on a wide range of situations.
   Question: Is every chapter in *¡Claro que sí* divided into 18 chapters? Or is it something else that is divided into 18 chapters? What is it? How do you know?

   _____

   _____

   _____

   _____

   _____

   _____

4. **Sentence:** By beginning a lesson with an overview of activities, it will ease the students' anxiety.
   Question: What will ease the students' anxiety? What does "it" in the second half of the sentence stand for?

   _____

   _____

   _____

   _____

   _____

   _____

5. **Sentence:** Fascinated by Egyptian art and history, the pyramids attract millions of tourists every year.
   Question: Who is fascinated by Egyptian art and history? What does the reader have to do to figure it out from this sentence?

   _____

   _____

   _____

   _____

   _____

   _____

SUMMARY: MISPLACED MODIFIERS

What		
Definition	*Types*	*Examples*
A **misplaced – or dangling – modifier** is a phrase or clause that is separated from the word it is supposed to modify or that modifies a word not clearly identified in a sentence. Misplaced modifiers include but are not limited to the list to the right.	*-ing phrases:*	*<u>Having set clear goals for the semester</u>, my study space is really important to achieve these goals. *I always use a dictionary when I come across an unfamiliar word, <u>helping me improve my vocabulary</u>.
	-ed phrases:	*<u>Frustrated by the unruly third graders</u>, the students threw spitballs at the teacher. *<u>Bored out of my mind</u>, the lesson dragged on and on without any breaks.
	Adjectives:	*<u>Unclear and convoluted</u>, the students could not understand the chapter. *<u>Cold from walking for hours in the snow</u>, the woodstove in the cabin was a welcome sight for the hikers.
	Prepositional phrases:	*<u>After hours of walking in the snow</u>, the woodstove in the cabin was a welcome sight for the hikers. *<u>With frequent headaches</u>, the doctor recommended additional tests and a CT scan.
	Relative (aka adjective) clauses:	*The escapees hid in the house in the woods **which had a secret basement**. *To fix the pipe we called a plumber **that was leaking**.

Why		
Clarity	*Problem*	*Example*
Misplaced modifiers are generally not a good thing. They create confusion and make it harder for your reader to understand what you are trying to say.	• They can perplex the reader as to who is doing what and cause the reader to go back and reread the sentence:	**Example:** *When testing my first participant, the four-year-old used diminutive suffixes at the end of each word.* **Source of confusion:** A four-year-old clearly can't test study participants, so who did the testing?
	• They can mislead the reader by inadvertently conveying the wrong information.	**Example:** Mike Duncan, an author and historian, conducted an interview with Dr. Daniel Quezada, who wrote the book *The Storm Before the Storm.* **Source of misinformation:** It is Mike Duncan, not Dr. Daniel Quezada, who wrote the book *The Storm Before the Storm.* Yet the placement of this relative clause makes it seem like Dr. Quezada is the author.
	• They can create an unintended humorous effect. If used for the specific purpose of such an effect, for example, in a comedy skit or a short story, misplaced modifiers can be an effective rhetorical tool. But if you do not want the reader to laugh, to be distracted from your main point, or to perceive you as an incompetent writer, you should avoid them.	**Examples:** • Having hiked in the snow for hours, the woodstove was a welcome sight at the cabin. • To fix the pipe we called the plumber that was leaking. **The source of (unintended) humor:** • The wood oven was not hiking in the snow, but the image the sentence creates is of an oven walking in the door and being happily met by those already in the cabin. • The plumber was not leaking. The pipe was. But a plumber with the water seeping out of them is a funny image.

How to Edit		
Type of Problem	*Steps*	*Examples*
Type 1: Misplaced modifiers	*Step 1: Identify which modifier causes the confusion.*	**Fascinated by Egyptian art and history**, the pyramids attract millions of tourists every year. **After hours of walking in the snow**, the woodstove in the cabin was a welcome sight for the hikers.
	Step 2: Decide which word the modifier is supposed to go with.	Fascinated by Egyptian art and history, the pyramids attract millions of **tourists** every year. After hours of walking in the snow, the woodstove in the cabin was a welcome sight for **the hikers**.
	Step 3: Move the modifier next to the word it goes with.	Every year, the pyramids attract millions of **tourists fascinated by Egyptian art and history**. **After hours of walking in the snow, the hikers** welcomed the sight of a woodstove in the cabin.
	Step 4: Check the revised sentence and make additional changes if necessary to keep the sentence coherent and flowing well with the sentence before it and after.	• Additional changes sometimes may be necessary in a sentence where a modifier is moved. • There are multiple ways to revise the same sentence after you move the modifier. **After hours of walking in the snow, the hikers** welcomed the sight of a woodstove in the cabin. OR The woodstove in the cabin was a welcome sight to the **hikers, who had walked for hours in the snow.** OR **Having walked in the snow for hours, the hikers** welcomed the sight of a woodstove in the cabin. **To the hikers, who had walked in the snow for hours,** the woodstove in the cabin was a welcome sight.

(Continued)

Type 2: Modified word is missing from the sentence	Step 1: Identify which modifier causes confusion.	**When testing my first participant**, the four-year-old used diminutive suffixes at the end of each word. **With frequent headaches**, the doctor recommended additional tests and a CT scan.
	Step 2: Decide which word or phrase the modifier is supposed to go with.	Who was testing the participant? – In this case, **the writer him- or herself**. Who had frequent headaches: the doctor or somebody else? – In this case, it would make sense for somebody else – **the patient** – to be having frequent headaches.
	Step 3: Insert the relevant word or phrase into the sentence. Make the necessary changes in the verb form.	When **I was testing** my first participant, a four-year old child, **I noticed** that she used diminutive suffixes at the end of each word. Because **the patient was having** frequent headaches, the doctor recommended additional tests and a CT scan.
	Step 4: Check the revised sentence and make additional changes if necessary to keep the sentence coherent and flowing well with the sentence before it and after.	• Additional changes sometimes may be necessary in a sentence where a word or phrase is inserted. • There are multiple ways to revise the same sentence after you insert the modified word or phrase. Because **the patient was having** frequent headaches, the doctor recommended additional tests and a CT scan. OR With **the patient having** frequent headaches, the doctor recommended additional tests and a CT scan. OR The doctor recommended additional tests and a CT scan to **the patient with frequent headaches.** OR The doctor recommended additional tests and a CT scan to **the patient who was having frequent headaches.**

(Continued)

Type 3: The word "it" that seems to refer to a modifier	*Step 1: Decide what the word "it" refers to.*	By beginning a lesson with an overview of activities, it will ease the students' anxiety. It was hard to understand the lecture, **having missed the previous week of class**.
	Step 2: Find the problematic modifier and turn it into a noun group or clause that can replace the word "it."	It = Beginning a lesson with an overview of activities It = ? Somebody missed the previous class. This somebody is a person. They cannot be referred to as "it." Possible replacements depend on the context.
	Step 3: Replace the word "it" with the newly formed noun group or clause.	**Beginning a lesson with an overview of activities** will ease the students' anxiety. **Having missed the previous week of class**, I was having a hard time understanding the lecture.
	Step 4: Check the revised sentence and make additional changes if necessary to keep the sentence coherent and flowing well with the sentence before it and after.	• Additional changes sometimes may be necessary in a sentence where a word or phrase is replaced. • There are multiple ways to revise the same sentence after you replace the word "it" that seems to refer to a modifier. **Having missed the previous week of class**, I was having a hard time understanding the lecture. OR **It was hard for me** to understand the lecture **because I missed the previous week of class**.

PRACTICE 5.2-B

 Directions: Editing

In this exercise you will practice detecting misplaced modifiers and correcting them. The sentences and passages below come from typical student essays in a variety of classes.

- Read each passage carefully.
- Identify a misplaced modifier and the element it is supposed to modify.
- Use one of the techniques in the table above to edit the sentences in such a way as to place the modifier in the appropriate place.

1. Before I was able to make any major decisions, I had to talk to my parents first. After telling my parents about the car, they recommended that I should wait until I had more money to buy a newer car.

   _____
   _____
   _____
   _____
   _____

2. Having a long-distance relationship, the distance affected both of us.

   _____
   _____
   _____
   _____
   _____

3. I was glad to have supportive people that influenced my decision. By having those influential people, they were able to persuade me to go to college.

   _____
   _____
   _____
   _____
   _____

4. By starting the chapter with a particular situation, the vocabulary and grammar rules are introduced in the dialogue and expanded upon within the chapter.

   _____

_____

5. Students are allowed to practice structure, and then allowed to come up with their own responses, helping them reinforce the new lesson.

_____

6. After observing the Spanish 1 class, several topics by Harmer also applied to the ethnographic notes that I took.

_____

7. By having the lessons on the board, it will remind the students of what needs to be accomplished by the end of the day.

_____

8. By reducing the hierarchical feeling of a classroom, students will be more self-confident and stimulated to learn.

_____

9. A student may be very focused, relaxed and motivated in learning the material, yet this individual may still have a high filter, thus hindering the language learning process.

_____

PRACTICE 5.2-C

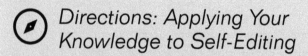

Directions: Applying Your Knowledge to Self-Editing

Now it is time to apply to your own writing the revision skills you've gained in this section. Select a section of a paper you wrote or are currently writing for any class – preferably something in your major. The passage should be about 300 words long or more.

- Read the passage carefully one sentence at a time.
- Stop after each sentence and examine it carefully.
- Misplaced modifiers often occur as introductory phrases. Check if the sentence has an introductory phrase.
- If the sentence has an introductory phrase, decide what the phrase is supposed to modify.
- If the modifier phrase is not placed next to the noun it is supposed to modify, revise the sentence.
- Reread the previous sentence, the revised sentence, and the next sentence together. Ensure that there is a smooth flow of meaning in the text.
- Make additional revisions if necessary.
- Reflect on the revisions you made. Did you have many problems to correct? What types of misplaced modifiers did you predominantly find in your own writing? How can you make sure you avoid them in the future?

5.3 HOW DO I CHOOSE THE RIGHT WORD FORMS?

After you work through this section of the chapter, you will be well on the way to say confidently:

◎ I can choose appropriately between closely related word forms.

◎ I can choose an appropriate word among many similarly sounding words.

PRACTICE 5.3-A

 Directions: Discovering Parts of Speech

The goals of this exercise are twofold. The first aim is to raise your awareness of how misusing parts of speech in the flow of writing can create confusion for the reader. The second aim is to focus your attention on how to replace the misused word forms (aka parts of speech) with the appropriate ones.

- The sentences below were written by students in first-year composition classes in college. Read each sentence carefully.
- Each sentence contains at least one error due to a misused part of speech.
- First, correct the error.
- Then, provide a short explanation of why you are replacing one word form with another.

Example

Student sentence: In each generation, the general population of *obese* increases drastically.

Correction: *In each generation, the general population of obese* **people** *increases drastically.*

OR In each generation, **the rates of obesity** *increase drastically among the general population.*

Explanation: *The word "obese" is an adjective. It cannot appear on its own. It needs to be used with a noun: obese people. That is why, in the first correction, I inserted the word "people" after "obese." Or it needs to be changed into a noun – "obesity." In the second correction, I used the noun "obesity" and added "the rates of" to make it clear and specific.*

1. At a fast-food restaurant, even ordering a healthy option often means consuming more than the daily recommending amount of calories in one meal.

    _____

    _____

    _____

    _____

    _____

2. When the author talks to his American friends about parenting, he is usually met with polite disbelieve.

    _____

    _____

    _____

    _____

    _____

3. The first step in choosing your major is to identity what interests you the most.

    _____

    _____

    _____

    _____

    _____

4. Time management is extremely important if you want to success in college.

    _____

    _____

    _____

    _____

    _____

5. Adolescents is the period of transition from being a child to being an adult.

    _____

    _____

    _____

    _____

    _____

6. There are many careers in sustainable urban developing for environmental engineers.

_____
_____
_____
_____
_____

7. Due to their stressful jobs, many people find it difficulty to relax at the end of the day.

_____
_____
_____
_____
_____

8. Our seafood offerings include such tasteful options as shrimp skewers, crab puffs, and fresh catch of the day.

_____
_____
_____
_____
_____

PRACTICE 5.3-B

 ## Directions: Practicing Word Forms

This exercise is designed to help you practice producing different forms of related words.

- The table below contains words randomly selected from the Academic Word List – a list of 570 words and their related forms that occur most frequently in academic writing.
- For each word, write in the missing related forms belonging to different parts of speech.[4] Keep in mind:
  - In some cases, more than one correct answer is possible.
  - **It will not be possible to find all three forms in all cases.**
- The first word has been done as an example.

Noun	Verb	Adjective
analysis	*analyze*	*analyzable*
category		
	demonstrate	
		emergent
	facilitate	
gender		
		hierarchical
intensity		
		manual
	persist	
	occur	
		normal
justification		
	validate	
		subsequent

PRACTICE 5.3-C

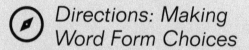

Directions: Making Word Form Choices

The purpose of this exercise is to practice choosing the context-appropriate word forms in a text.

- The text below is an excerpt from a Wikipedia article. Read the text carefully.
- Then select one word form from the three offered in each parenthesis to fit the context better.
- Discuss with a partner why you are making each choice.

Text:

From: https://en.wikipedia.org/wiki/World_Heritage_Site

World Heritage Sites: The Origin

In 1954, the government of Egypt decided to build the new Aswan High Dam, whose resulting future reservoir would eventually inundate a large stretch of the Nile valley containing (1) (<u>culture/cultural/cultured</u>) treasures of ancient Egypt and ancient Nubia. In 1959, the governments of Egypt and Sudan requested UNESCO to assist them to (2) (<u>protect/protected/protection</u>) and rescue the endangered monuments and sites. In 1960, the Director-General of UNESCO launched the International Campaign to Save the Monuments of Nubia. This appeal resulted in the excavation and recording of hundreds of sites, the recovery of thousands of objects, as well as the salvage and relocation to higher ground of several (3) (<u>import/important/importance</u>) temples. The most famous of these are the temple complexes of Abu Simbel and Philae. The campaign ended in 1980 and was (4) (<u>consider/considerable/considered</u>) a success. To thank countries which especially contributed to the campaign's (5) (<u>succeed/successful/success</u>), Egypt donated four temples; the Temple of Dendur was moved to the Metropolitan Museum of Art in New York City, the Temple of Debod to the Parque del Oeste in Madrid, the Temple of Taffeh to the Rijksmuseum van Oudheden in Leiden, and the Temple of Ellesyia to Museo Egizio in Turin.

The (6) (<u>project/projection/projectile</u>) cost US$80 million (equivalent to $251.28 million in 2020), about $40 million of which was (7) (<u>collection/collected/collect</u>) from 50 countries. The project's success led to other safeguarding campaigns, such as saving Venice and its lagoon in Italy, the ruins of Mohenjo-daro in Pakistan, and the Borobodur Temple Compounds in Indonesia. Together with the International Council on Monuments and Sites, UNESCO then (8) (<u>initial/initiation/initiated</u>) a draft convention to protect cultural heritage.

PRACTICE 5.3-D

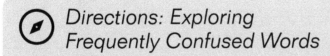

Directions: Exploring Frequently Confused Words

The purpose of this practice is to identify words that are commonly mixed up by writers. These words often sound nearly identical, but have different meanings, so they can cause confusion for readers.

- Read each pair of sentences carefully.
- Look up the bold-faced words in a dictionary. Do it even if you think you know what the words mean.
- Write the "rule" for using the bold-faced words.
- Write your own example sentences for each of the bold-faced words.

Example

Pair:

1. If students do not take a sufficient number of science classes in high school, universities are compelled to **<u>accept</u>** less qualified applicants for STEM majors.
2. There is little evidence of market integration, **<u>except</u>** between South Korea and Japan markets.

Rule:

Use the verb "accept" when you mean "willingly receive something that somebody gives you."

Use "except" to mean "excluding." "Except" is usually a preposition.

Own example sentences:

1. *We **accept** all qualified students.*
2. *<u>I didn't eat anything **except** a donut.</u>*

Pair 1:

a. Abstract words might **<u>affect</u>** the ease of understanding the text.
b. We investigated the **<u>effect</u>** of aid on the economic growth in developing countries.

Rule:

_____

_____

_____

_____

_____

Own examples:

_____

_____

_____

_____

Pair 2:

a. The error remained on the record decade after decade, frequently **cited** by government officials, media, and even scholars without any critical analysis.
b. A group was defined as a cluster of dolphins **sighted** by the observer in close proximity to each other and engaged in similar behaviors.

Rule:

_____

_____

_____

_____

_____

Own examples:

_____

_____

_____

_____

Pair 3:

a. This type of performance never fails to **elicit** applause.
b. The deadly fentanyl, an **illicit** drug, has claimed yet another young life.

Rule:

_____

_____

_____

_____

_____

Own examples:

_____

_____

_____

_____

Pair 4:

a. These stars, the so-called red giants, then begin to **lose** material
    to the space.
b. The water weakens glaciers and causes icebergs to break **loose**.

Rule:

_____

_____

_____

_____

_____

Own examples:

_____

_____

_____

_____

Pair 5:

a. Each participant was interviewed twice, once alone and once in
    the presence of **their** partner.
b. The friends know that **they're** being followed.

Rule:

_____

_____

_____
_____
_____

Own examples:

_____
_____
_____
_____

Pair 6:

a. When we first started on the project, we just kind of **threw** ideas around until we stumbled on a gem of one.
b. We then went **through** the process of moving the data to the central archive.

Rule:

_____
_____
_____
_____
_____

Own examples:

_____
_____
_____
_____

PRACTICE 5.3-E

 Directions: Editing

In this exercise, you will continue to explore frequently confused words. Your work will focus on editing writing for appropriate word choices. All passages below have been adapted from the work of students in first-year composition classes.

- Read each passage carefully.
- All passages contain at least one misused word. Your task is to correct the misused word and provide an explanation for the correction.
- The first sentence is done for you as an example.
- In passages 2–4, the misused word has been identified and corrected. You need to provide an explanation for the correction.
- In passages 5–7, the misused word has been identified but not corrected. You need to correct it and provide an explanation for the correction.
- In passages 8–10, the word has not been identified. It is your task to find it, correct it, and provide an explanation for your correction.

Example
Passage 1:

The reason for many immigrants to come to the U.S. is because they want a better life for themselves and their children, and ~~are~~ **our** nation provides them with many opportunities to move up.

Explanation:

*"Are" is a linking verb. It links the subject with something that describes the subject – "Immigrants **are** here to seek better opportunities." "Our" indicates possession. Because we talk about a nation that belongs to us, the word should be "our."*

Passage 2:

Immigration is mostly ~~effecting~~ **affecting** the service and agriculture industries since these two industries employ a lot of immigrants.

Explanation:

_____
_____
_____
_____
_____

Passage 3:
Many pilots have to build their flight time for a year or more because ~~its~~ it's not a small number.

Explanation:

_____

_____

_____

_____

_____

Passage 4:
The old adage of the service industry is that the ~~costumer~~ customer is always right. But this attitude of managers is damaging to the ~~moral~~ morale of retail workers.

Explanation:

_____

_____

_____

_____

_____

Passage 5:
A pilot who has received a multi-engine rating can fly airplanes that have more than one engine, which are much safer **then** single-engine planes.

Correction and explanation:

_____

_____

_____

_____

_____

Passage 6:
Some of the **principals** of an efficient welfare program are sustainability, collaboration of the state and local state, and effective communication between each poor family, staff and bureaucrats.

Correction and explanation:

_____

_____

_____

_____

_____

Passage 7:

Solar energy has a lot of advantages. It is easily available, eco-friendly, abundant, and inexhaustible. However, despite being a better choice than coal or oil, solar energy also has some **downfalls**.

Correction and explanation:

_____
_____
_____
_____
_____

Passage 8:
Humans often buy cosmetic products without considering how each company tests the chemicals. Companies that do not use animal testing are still effective in insuring the safety of their cosmetics.

Correction and explanation:

_____
_____
_____
_____
_____

Passage 9:
The price and portability of computers have improved significantly in the passed two decades, while demand for computer access has skyrocketed.

Correction and explanation:

_____
_____
_____
_____
_____

Passage 10:
As the popularity and utility of computers increased, a variety of new health problems arose. One cause of these problems was that people were spending to much time in front of the screen.

Correction and explanation:

_____
_____
_____
_____
_____

NOTES

1 Temming, M. (2021, May 20). Watch this beautiful, high-resolution simulation of how stars are born. *Science News.* www.sciencenews.org/article/starforge-star-formation-simulation

2 Temming, M. (2021, May 20). "Tree farts" contribute about a fifth of greenhouse gasses from ghost forests. *Science News.* www.sciencenews.org/article/ghost-forest-tree-farts-emissions-greenhouse-gases

3 Conover, E. (2021, May 13). A study of Earth's crust hints that supernovas aren't gold mines. *Science News.* www.sciencenews.org/article/supernova-heavy-elements-source-earth-crust-deep-sea

4 Coxhead, A. (2000). A new academic word list. *TESOL Quarterly, 34*(2), 213–238.

Appendix A: Editing for Subject-Verb Agreement

Subject-verb agreement is a principle stating that properties of the subject of the sentence must match the properties of its verb. In practice, it means that singular subjects must have singular verbs. Because in English, the "singular" is only reflected in the present tense verbs, it is only with the present tense verbs that we must ensure the agreement.

This step-by-step guide will help you edit your sentences for subject-verb agreement.

Step 1: Find all the verbs in the sentence

A significant amount of research in urban science <u>is informed</u> by the notion that cities <u>are</u> complex dynamic systems.

Step 2: Ask: *Who/What is doing the action of the verb?*

What is informed by the notion that cities are complex dynamic systems? – *A significant amount of research in urban science.*

What is/are complex dynamic systems? – *Cities.*

The answer to this question is the subject of each verb.

Step 3: Draw an arrow from each verb to its subject

A significant amount of research in urban science <u>is informed</u> by

the notion that cities <u>are</u> complex dynamic systems.

Step 4: Decide if the main word in the subject refers to a singular concept or a plural one

A significant <u>amount</u> of research in urban science is informed by the notion that <u>cities</u> are complex dynamic systems.

Amount – singular (one thing, one amount)

Cities – plural (multiple things)

Step 5: Check if the verb matches the subject in number

(A significant) <u>*amount*</u> *(of research in urban science)* <u>*is*</u> *informed...* – both singular

Cities are – both plural

Step 6: If you find a mismatch, adjust the agreement:

Scenario A: You used the singular form of the subject and the plural form of the verb, but you meant for the subject to be plural. Fix the subject to the plural form and keep the plural verb.

Original: **Both historical and social <u>perspective</u> have been adopted in this analysis.*

Correction: *Both historical and social <u>perspectives</u> have been adopted in this analysis.*

Scenario B: You used a plural verb with a singular subject. The subject refers to one thing or a thing that cannot be counted, and this is exactly what you mean. Fix the verb.

Original: ** A historical perspective <u>have</u> been adopted in this analysis.*

Correction: *A historical perspective <u>has</u> been adopted in this analysis.*

SAMPLE EDITING WORK-THROUGH

The passage below is a sample adapted from student writing. We will work through it as a model for your own editing following the steps outlined above.

Remember: in your own editing, you do not need to create any tables. You can work directly with your text and put the necessary notes on the margins. The table below is a representation of the reasoning process you should be going through, not the actual physical format of how you should be doing it. As such, you can combine Steps 2 and 3, for example and mark the arrows as you ask who performs the action of the verb and find the verb's subject(s).

Another thing to keep in mind is that when you first go through this editing process, it may take a long time. But as you practice and become more observant, three things will happen:

1. You will get more efficient and faster.
2. You will be able to combine more editing steps into one action because they will become automatic.
3. You will make fewer errors in the first place, so there will be less to correct.

Step 1: Find all the verbs.
Good advertisements <u>can convince</u> people <u>to purchase</u> products they <u>are advertising</u>. Good advertising <u>let</u> companies <u>earn</u> more money. For example, Progressive, an insurance company, <u>has made</u> their advertisements fun and informative. People who <u>see</u> a lot of Progressive advertisements on TV really <u>like</u> this company and <u>buy</u> their car insurance from them. Progressive commercials shown on TV always <u>represents</u> a bright background, <u>making</u> people feel bright and cheerful too. Each commercial <u>shows</u> a conversation between customers and a Progressive salesperson dressed in a white shirt with a blue Progressive logo on it. In one commercial, the salesperson <u>prints</u> out a very long list of discounts for the customers, who <u>need</u> a big bag to take them away. Progressive advertisements <u>are</u> not only funny and interesting, but also <u>provides</u> lots of useful information about discounts and lower auto insurance rates. Also, in the advertisements, the cashier always <u>mention</u> the company's website. On the website, you <u>can get</u> your own quote for all kinds of insurance within just six minutes, such as insurance for cars, motorcycles, and even homes by simply <u>typing</u> in your information. You <u>can also compare</u> the rate at Progressive with rates at other companies. Because Progressive <u>has</u> fun and informative advertisements, they <u>attract</u> a lot of customers, which <u>bring</u> it a lot of profit. Progressive <u>is</u> a good example of how good advertising <u>can make</u> a company a lot of money.

Step 2: Ask who is doing the action of the verb.	
	Editing notes
What or what <u>can convince</u> people? – <u>Good advertisements</u>.	"Can" does not need to agree with the subject. Nothing to fix here.
Who will be doing the <u>purchasing</u>? – <u>People</u>.	"to purchase" does not need to agree with the subject. Nothing to fix here.
Who <u>is/are advertising</u> products? – <u>They</u> (good advertisements).	Both the subject and the verb in the text are plural ("are" is a plural form; "is" is singular). Nothing to fix here.
Who or what <u>lets</u> companies earn more money? – <u>Good advertising</u>.	-ing subjects need a singular verb → *add -s*
Who is allowed to <u>earn</u> more money? – <u>Companies</u>.	"earn" here does not need to agree with "companies" because it comes after the verb "let," which takes a bare form after it.

(Continued)

Who <u>has made</u> their advertisements fun and informative? – Progressive, an insurance company.	Both the subject and the verb are singular. The verb needs to have an -s (has), which it already has. Nothing to fix here.
Who <u>sees</u> a lot of Progressive advertisements? – People.	Both the subject and the verb are plural. No -s is needed. Nothing to fix here.
Who likes the company and <u>buys</u> their insurance from them? – People.	The subject and the verbs are plural. No -s is needed. Nothing to fix here.
Who always <u>represents</u> the bright background? – Progressive <u>commercials</u> on TV.	The subject is plural (many commercials), but the verb has an -s. Because the subject needs to remain plural → *remove the -s from the verb.*
What <u>makes</u> people bright and cheerful? – <u>Commercials</u>.	-ing verbs – like "making" – with no helping verbs and with the subject in a different clause do not need to agree with the subject. Nothing to fix here.
What <u>shows</u> a conversation between customers and a salesperson? – <u>Each commercial</u>.	Subjects with the word "each" in them are always singular. The verb must be singular too. Nothing to fix here.
Who <u>prints</u> a long list of discounts? – <u>The salesperson</u>.	Both the subject and the verb should remain singular. Nothing to fix here.
Who <u>needs</u> a big bag to carry a printout of discounts away? – <u>Customers</u>.	Both the subject and the verb in the text are plural. Nothing to fix here.
What <u>is/are</u> funny and interesting? – <u>Progressive advertisements</u>.	The subject is plural. The verb in the actual sentence is "are," which is also plural. Nothing to fix here.
What <u>provides</u> lots of useful information? – <u>Progressive advertisements</u>.	The subject is plural (many advertisements). But the verb in the text has an -s. *The -s needs to be removed* to match the verb to the plural subject.
Who <u>mentions</u> the company website? – <u>The cashier</u>.	There is only one cashier. The verb in the text needs an -s. → *Add the -s to the verb.*
Who <u>can get</u> one's own quote? – <u>You</u>.	"Can" does not need to agree with the subject. Nothing to fix here.

(Continued)

Who might be doing the <u>typing</u>? – <u>You</u>.	-ing verbs – like "typing" – with no helping verbs and with the subject in a different clause do not need to agree with the subject. Nothing to fix here.
Who <u>can compare</u> the rates? – <u>You</u>.	"Can" does not need to agree with the subject. Nothing to fix here.
Who <u>has</u> fun and informative advertisements? – <u>Progressive</u>.	Both the subject and the verb in the text are singular. Nothing to fix here.
Who attracts a lot of customers? – They.	Even though the word "they" refers to the company "Progressive," the word itself is plural. Therefore, the verb has to be plural too. Nothing to fix here.
What or who brings Progressive a lot of profit? – The answer is not clear here. It may be the "customers" or it may be the ability of Progressive to attract a lot of customers.	Two possible fixes: 1. If the writer means that the customers bring Progressive a lot of profit, the writer needs to <u>change the word "which" to the word "who"</u> because customers are people and cannot be referred to by the word "which." In this case, *the verb needs to stay the same because "customers" is plural.* 2. If it is the ability to attract customers that brings Progressive profit, then the word "which" refers to the whole idea, not just one noun group. Such "which" always needs a singular verb, so *-s needs to be added to "bring" → "brings."* 3. *In either case, the writer needs to make some revisions to the sentence to make it clear.*
What <u>is</u> a good example? – <u>Progressive</u>.	Both the subject and the verb in the text are singular. Nothing to be fixed here.

(Continued)

What <u>can make</u> a company a lot of money? – <u>Good advertising</u>.	"Can" does not need to agree with the subject. Nothing to fix here.

Step 3: Draw arrows from each verb to its subject.

Good advertisements <u>can convince</u> people <u>to purchase</u> products they <u>are advertising</u>. Good advertising <u>let</u>

companies <u>earn</u> more money. For example, Progressive, an insurance company, <u>has made</u> their advertisements

fun and informative. People who <u>see</u> a lot of Progressive advertisements on TV really <u>like</u> this company and <u>buy</u>

their car insurance from them. Progressive commercials shown on TV always <u>represents</u> a bright background,

<u>making</u> people feel bright and cheerful too. Each commercial <u>shows</u> a conversation between customers and a

Progressive salesperson dressed in a white shirt with a blue Progressive logo on it. In one commercial, the

<u>salesperson</u> <u>prints</u> out a very long list of discounts for the customers, who <u>need</u> a big bag to take them away.

Progressive advertisements <u>are</u> not only funny and interesting, but also <u>provides</u> lots of useful information

about discounts and lower auto insurance rates. Also, in the advertisements, the <u>cashier always mention</u> the

company's website. On the website, you <u>can get</u> your own quote for all kinds of insurance within just six

minutes, such as insurance for cars, motorcycles, and even homes by simply <u>typing</u> in your information. You <u>can</u>

<u>also compare</u> the rate at Progressive with rates at other companies. Because Progressive <u>has</u> fun and

informative advertisements, they <u>attract</u> a lot of customers, which <u>bring</u> it a lot of profit. Progressive <u>is</u> a good

example of how good advertising <u>can make</u> a company a lot of money.

Step 4: Check if the main word in the subject refers to a singular or plural concept.

See the editing notes for Step 2 above.

Step 5: Check if the subject and the verb match each other in number.

See the editing notes for Step 2 above.

Step 6: If you find a mismatch, fix the agreement as necessary.

Good advertisements <u>can convince</u> people <u>to purchase</u> products they <u>are advertising</u>. Good advertising <u>lets</u> companies <u>earn</u> more money. For example, Progressive, an insurance company, <u>has made</u> their advertisements fun and informative. People who <u>see</u> a lot of Progressive advertisements on TV really <u>like</u> this company and <u>buy</u> their car insurance from them. Progressive commercials shown on TV always <u>presents</u> a bright background, <u>making</u> people feel bright and cheerful too. Each commercial <u>shows</u> a conversation between customers and a Progressive salesperson dressed in a white shirt with a blue Progressive logo on it. In one commercial, the salesperson <u>prints</u> out a very long list of discounts for the customers, who <u>need</u> a big bag to take them away. Progressive advertisements <u>are</u> not only funny and interesting, but also <u>provides</u> lots of useful information about discounts and lower auto insurance rates. Also, in the advertisements, the cashier always <u>mentions</u> the company's website. On the website, you <u>can get</u> your own quote for all kinds of insurance within just six minutes, such as insurance for cars, motorcycles, and even homes by simply <u>typing</u> in your information. You <u>can also compare</u> the rate at Progressive with rates at other companies. Because Progressive <u>has</u> fun and informative advertisements, they <u>attract</u> a lot of customers, which <u>brings</u> it a lot of profit. Progressive <u>is</u> a good example of how good advertising <u>can make</u> a company a lot of money.

OR:

Because Progressive <u>has</u> fun and informative advertisements, they <u>attract</u> a lot of customers, **who** <u>bring</u> it a lot of profit. Progressive <u>is</u> a good example of how good advertising <u>can make</u> a company a lot of money.

Appendix B: Editing for Verb Tense Consistency

The principle of verb tense consistency means that the writer must use the same verb forms – past or present – in a stretch of text that remains in one time frame. When the need to switch the time frame – and the verb forms/tenses – arises, the writer must signal such a switch to the reader through the use of particular signal phrases or rhetorical moves.

What do we mean by "time frame"? We mean this:

1. When we make a generalization, provide definitions, report research findings that are current or that we agree with, state our current opinions, relate regularly occurring events, or present timeless facts, we write in the **present tense**.
2. When we give specific examples, tell a story, report outdated research findings or the research findings we expect to argue against, we write in the **past tense**.
3. When we switch from the present to the past time frame, we must signal to the reader that we are about to do so. We signal the shift through:
   a. Time phrases (e.g., *in 1986*, or *when I was a child*, or *after the completion of the project*, etc.)
   b. Markers of shifts in the purpose of the following text (e.g., *for example*, or *generally speaking*, or *to conclude*, or *on the whole*, etc.)
   c. Using a bridging verb tense, such as present perfect or present perfect progressive (e.g., *While corporal punishment **was** common in schools in the past, the attitudes towards it **have been changing**, and currently, few states **allow** corporal punishment of children in public schools*).

This step-by-step guide will help you edit your sentences for subject-verb agreement. Because verb tense consistency must be edited at the level of a paragraph rather than a single sentence, a sample editing work-through is incorporated into the guide rather than being presented after it. The text used for the guide (and the work-through) has been adapted from student writing.

Step 1: Read your text aloud and underline or highlight every complete verb.

Reminder: A complete verb is a verb that either shows the time the action happens/happened or has a helping verb in front of it, or both:

Evidence <u>suggests</u> that <u>reading</u> to young children for at least 20 minutes a day <u>may improve</u> their vocabulary.

- Suggests – complete verb (has an -s at the end; means present time)
- Reading – incomplete verb (has -ing at the end but no helping verb; does not indicate any particular time; reading can happen in the past, present, or future)
- May improve – complete verb (has the helping verb *may* in front of the lexical verb *improve*)

Positive thinking **is** a very powerful tool because it **can help** people overcome trouble and obstacles. What **is** positive thinking? It **is** an attitude that **revolves** around noticing and anticipating the good in one's life. It **is** an attitude that **makes** one expect that everything **will turn** out for the best. I **have** a good example of how positive thinking **helped** me overcome troubles in my life. A few years ago, I **decide** to go back to school and earn my Associate degree. My husband **did not want** me to do that. He **wants** me to stay on my job and then come home and take care of the house and the kids. We **started** to argue a lot. But my job **was** hard and **does not pay** enough money. And I **am** too tired after work to take care of the household, but my husband **doesn't help** because his job **is** also hard and he **is** also tired. Even though it **is** hard, I **was thinking** positively. I **know** that after I **finish** my Associate degree, I **could get** a better job. So I **persevered**. I **told** my husband that when I **finish** my Associate degree, I **can get** a promotion and get more money. I **was expecting** that our life will get better. I **was** right. After I **finish** my degree, my boss **gave** me a promotion and a raise. She also **gave** me a flexible schedule so that I **could transfer** to a four-year college. I **am** now **attending** a four-year college part time, and I **am making** more money than I **was** before. My husband finally **saw** the benefit of me getting an Associate degree. But I **would** never **keep going** with it without positive thinking. My story **was** a good example of how positive thinking **can help** people overcome difficulties and lead to a better life.

Step 2: Identify the purposes of each section of the text or paragraph, i.e., the jobs that each section of the text is supposed to be doing.

Text	Purpose/Job
Positive thinking **is** a very powerful tool because it **can help** people overcome trouble and obstacles. What **is** positive thinking? It **is** an attitude that **revolves** around noticing and anticipating the good in one's life. It **is** an attitude that **makes** one expect that everything **will turn** out for the best. I **have** a good example of how positive thinking **helped** me overcome troubles in my life.	Generalization and definition of positive thinking. An opinion or claim about positive thinking
A few years ago, I **decide** to go back to school and earn my Associate degree. My husband **did not want** me to do that. He **wants** me to stay on my job and then come home and take care of the house and the kids. We **started** to argue a lot. But my job **was** hard and **does not pay** enough money. And I **am** too tired after work to take care of the household, but my husband **doesn't help** because his job **is** also hard and he **is** also tired. Even though it **is** hard, I **was thinking** positively. I **know** that after I **finish** my Associate degree, I **could get** a better job. So I **persevered**. I **told** my husband that when I **finish** my Associate degree, I **can get** a promotion and get more money. I **was expecting** that our life will get better. I **was** right. After I **finish** my degree, my boss **gave** me a promotion and a raise. She also **gave** me a flexible schedule so that I **could transfer** to a four-year college. I **am** now **attending** a four-year college part time, and I **am making** more money than I **was** before. My husband finally **saw** the benefit of me getting an Associate degree. But I **would** never **keep going** with it without positive thinking.	Specific example – a story that already happened
My story **was** a good example of how positive thinking **can help** people overcome difficulties and lead to a better life.	Conclusion and generalization from the example

Step 3: Determine the primary time frame that each section should be in.

Text	Purpose/Job	Time frame
Positive thinking **is** a very powerful tool because it **can help** people overcome trouble and obstacles. What **is** positive thinking? It **is** an attitude that **revolves** around noticing and anticipating the good in one's life. It **is** an attitude that **makes** one expect that everything **will turn** out to the best. I **have** a good example of how positive thinking **helped** me overcome troubles in my life.	Generalization and definition	Present or future
A few years ago, I **decide** to go back to school and earn my Associate degree. My husband **did not want** me to do that. He **wants** me to stay on my job and then come home and take care of the house and the kids. We **started** to argue a lot. But my job **was** hard and **does not pay** enough money. And I **am** too tired after work to take care of the household, but my husband **doesn't help** because his job **is** also hard and he **is** also tired. Even though it **is** hard, I **was thinking** positively. I **know** that after I **finish** my Associate degree, I **could get** a better job. So I **persevered**. I **told** my husband that when I **finish** my Associate degree, I **can get** a promotion and get more money. I **was expecting** that our life will get better. I **was** right. After I **finish** my degree, my boss **gave** me a promotion and a raise. She also **gave** me a flexible schedule so that I **could transfer** to a four-year college. I **am** now **attending** a four-year college part time, and I **am making** more money than I **was** before. My husband finally **saw** the benefit of me getting an Associate degree. But I **would** never **keep going** with it without positive thinking.	Specific example	Past tense
My story **was** a good example of how positive thinking **can help** people overcome difficulties and lead to a better life.	Conclusion and generalization from the example	Present tense

Step 4: Read through each section and identify the verbs that do not match the preferred time frame.

Text	Non-Matching Verbs
Positive thinking **is** a very powerful tool because it **can help** people overcome trouble and obstacles. What **is** positive thinking? It **is** an attitude that **revolves** around noticing and anticipating the good in one's life. It **is** an attitude that **makes** one expect that everything **will turn** out to the best. I **have** a good example of how positive thinking (helped) me overcome troubles in my life.	Everything is in the preferred present tense but "helped" is in the past tense. Needs to be changed.
A few years ago, I decide to go back to school and earn my Associate degree. My husband **did not want** me to do that. He wants me to stay on my job and then come home and take care of the house and the kids. We started to argue a lot. But my job **was** hard and does not pay enough money. And I am too tired after work to take care of the household, but my husband doesn't help because his job **is** also hard and he **is** also tired. Even though it **is** hard, I **was thinking** positively. I know that after I finish my Associate degree, I could get a better job. So I **persevered**. I told my husband that when I finish my Associate degree, I can get a promotion and get more money. I **was expecting** that our life will get better. I **was** right. After I finish my degree, my boss **gave** me a promotion and a raise. She also gave me a flexible schedule so that I **could transfer** to a four-year college. I am now **attending** a four-year college part time, and **I am making** more money than I **was** before. My husband finally **saw** the benefit of me getting an Associate degree. But I would never keep going with it without positive thinking.	There are a lot of switches between past and present. This section will need to be edited one verb at a time.
My story (was) a good example of how positive thinking **can help** people overcome difficulties and lead to a better life.	The first verb is in the past tense, but the rest is in the preferred present tense.

Step 5: Make changes to one verb at a time.

Corrected text	Explanations
Positive thinking is a very powerful tool because it can help people overcome trouble and obstacles. What is positive thinking? It is an attitude that revolves around noticing and anticipating the good in one's life. It is an attitude that makes one expect that everything will turn out to the best. I have a good example of how positive thinking **has helped** me overcome troubles in my life.	"Helped" needs to be in the present time frame, but the action already happened → change to "has helped" (have/has + Verb-ed/en; present perfect).

(Continued)

A few years ago, I **decided** to go back to school and earn my Associate degree. My husband did not want me to do that. He **wanted** me to stay on my job and then come home and take care of the house and the kids. We started to argue a lot. But my job was hard and **did not pay** enough money. And I **was** too tired after work to take care of the household, but my husband **didn't help** because his job **was** also hard and he **was** also tired. Even though it was hard, I was thinking positively. I **knew** that after I **finished** my Associate degree, I could get a better job. So I persevered. I told my husband that when I **finished** my Associate degree, I **could get** a promotion and get more money. I was expecting that our life will get better. I was right. After I **finished** my degree, my boss gave me a promotion and a raise. She also gave me a flexible schedule so that I could transfer to a four-year college.	"A few years ago" is a time phrase, introducing events that already happened. Everything after it should be in the simple past tense, even if some of it is still true in the present. The verb tense consistency must be maintained. Leave the past tense verbs as is and change the present tense ones into the past.
I am now attending a four-year college part time, and I am making more money than I was before. My husband finally **has seen** the benefit of me getting an Associate degree.	This is still the same example, but the time frame changes to "now" – the time phrase "now" is in the first sentence of this passage. This time phrase indicates that everything in this sentence must be in the present tense. If a past-time time phrase is used (such as "before"), the verb can be in the past tense. Change "saw" to "has seen" because the time frame must be present, but the action already happened.
But I **would** never **have kept going** with it without positive thinking.	This sentence takes the reader back to what was happening before now, so the verb needs to be shifted into the hypothetical past: Change "would keep going" to "would have kept going."
My story **is** a good example of how positive thinking can help people overcome difficulties and lead to a better life.	This is a conclusion, so it needs to be in the present tense. Change "was" to "is."

(Continued)

Step 6: Read the whole corrected text aloud again to make sure you've caught and fixed all the inconsistencies.

Why is it important to read aloud, and not silently?

When we read silently, our eyes skim over the words, and our brains perceive what we think **should** be in the text instead of what actually **is** in the text. Thus, reading silently, just with our eyes, makes us miss any errors there might be in our writing, especially if they are small errors, like a missing verb ending or an extra verb ending that shouldn't be there.

If we read aloud, our brains force our ears to hear what is actually written in the text. Hearing ourselves makes it easier to catch errors and typos. In other words, we can hear and notice what actually **is** there instead of what **should** be there. Therefore, we can correct any problems we catch this way.

Appendix C: Editing for Punctuation

Punctuation is very important in writing because it helps clarify the meaning the writer is trying to convey to the reader, to arrange the ideas in the most transparent way, to guide the reader through the organization and main points of the written piece. In formal writing in American English, punctuation rules are few and rather straightforward.

This step-by-step editing guide will help you edit your sentences for proper punctuation and make your writing clear and fluent.

Step 1: Read your text aloud and bracket all the clauses – i.e., stretches of written language with their own subjects and verbs.

[When an animal is in danger], [its hypothalamic-pituitary-adrenal system kicks in], [and a set of various hormones is released into the animal's body].

Step 2: Highlight or circle all the FANBOYS between clauses or at the beginning of clauses.

[When an animal is in danger], [its hypothalamic-pituitary-adrenal system kicks in], [and a set of various hormones is released into the animal's body].

Step 3: Check if the clauses on both sides of each FANBOY are complete independent clauses. If yes, make sure there is a comma in front of the FANBOY.

... [its hypothalamic-pituitary-adrenal system kicks in], [and a set of various hormones is released into the animal's body].

[Everyone on the planet experiences stress], [but they don't always notice it immediately.]

Step 4: Circle or highlight all the subordinating words at the beginning of the bracketed clauses (*when*, *because*, *if*, *after*, *before*, *that*, etc.).

[(When) *an animal is in danger*], [*its hypothalamic-pituitary-adrenal system kicks in*]...

Step 5: Check if the clause with the subordinator in it comes before or after the main clause. If it is before the main clause, put a comma after it. If it is after the main clause, make sure there is <u>no</u> comma before it.

[(When) *an animal is in* (danger)], [(its) *hypothalamic-pituitary-adrenal system kicks in*]...

Subordinate clause →   Main clause

[*In situations of constant stress, the brain begins to perceive stress all the time*] [(even) *if the actual stressor is not present*].

Main clause →   Subordinate clause

Step 6: Highlight or circle all instances of "who" or "which" at the beginning of clauses.

[*A chronically stressed body then turns into a feedback loop*] [*in* (which) *stress response goes out of control*].

[*Poor sleep,* (which) *often results from stress*], *contributes to this feedback loop*].

[*People* (who) *face a high level of chronic stress at work*] *are in danger of dying at a younger age*].

[*Dr. Edwards,* (who) *studied stress in college freshmen*], *suggests a series of relaxation strategies to relieve anxiety*].

Step 7: Determine if the clause starting with "which" or "who" adds something essential to the noun group it describes, or if it describes something or somebody unique.

[*A chronically stressed body then turns into a feedback loop*] [*in* (which) *stress response goes out of control*]. ← something essential (one of many loops, the kind that increases stress response)

[Poor sleep, (which) often results from stress], contributes to this feedback loop]. ← something unique (poor sleep as a whole)

[People (who) face a high level of chronic stress at work] are in danger of dying at a younger age]. ← something essential (only some of the people, the ones who face high levels of stress)

[Dr. Edwards, (who) studied stress in college freshmen], suggests a series of relaxation strategies to relieve anxiety]. ← somebody unique (the name of a specific individual person)

Step 8: Add (or keep) the commas around "who" and "which" clauses that describe something unique. Do not add (or delete) commas around "who" or "which" clauses that add essential information.

[A chronically stressed body then turns into a feedback loop] [in which stress response goes out of control]. ← something essential (one of many loops, the kind that increases stress response)

[Poor sleep, [which often results from stress], contributes to this feedback loop]. ← something unique (poor sleep as a whole)

[People [who face a high level of chronic stress at work] are in danger of dying at a younger age]. ← something essential (only some of the people, the ones who face high levels of stress)

[Dr. Edwards, [who studied stress in college freshmen], suggests a series of relaxation strategies to relieve anxiety]. ← somebody unique (the name of a specific individual person)

Step 9: If you find a segment that does not express a complete idea, but it is punctuated like a complete sentence, join it to another sentence.

[When negative emotions are chronic.] [The body begins experiencing a constant state of fight or flight.]

Incomplete idea

[When negative emotions are chronic], [the body begins experiencing a constant state of fight or flight].

Step 10: Reread the text aloud again to make sure that it flows smoothly and that you did not miss any punctuation problems.

SAMPLE EDITING WORK-THROUGH

The passage below is a sample adapted from student writing. We will work through it as a model for your own editing following the steps outlined above.

Remember: in your own editing, you do not need to create any tables. You can work directly with your text and put the necessary notes in the margins. The table below is a representation of the reasoning process you should be going through, not the actual physical format of how you should be doing it.

Another thing to keep in mind is that when you first go through this editing process, it may take a long time. But as you practice and become more observant, three things will happen:

1. You will get more efficient and faster.
2. You will be able to combine more editing steps into one action because they will become automatic.
3. You will make fewer punctuation errors in the first place, so there will be less to correct.

Step 1: Read the text aloud and bracket all clauses.
[The article states] [that everyone on the planet experiences stress]. [Stress in every shape and form is bad for people] [because it can kill]. [The first scientist [who uncovered the relationship between stress and health] was Hans Selye]. [This was back in early 20th century]. [Selye found] [that stress is linked to the perception of danger in our lives]. For example, [when animals are being hunted] [they get a rush of stress] [which allows them to run away to safety] [or they can fight for their life].
[At first, doctors doubted] [that stress had any effect on the physical body], [but in the 1950s, medical scientists discovered] [that stress can cause coronary disease]. [Basing their studies on people with different personalities]. [They discovered] [that the body was in the constant state of fight-or-flight], [if the person was always angry]. [This condition resulted in health problems]. [Stress is inevitable] [but there are ways to control it], [and the first thing [one must do] is not to be angry].

Steps 2 and 3: Highlight all FANBOYS and determine if the clauses on both sides of them are independent.	
Text	**Editing Notes**
[The article states] [that everyone on the planet experiences stress]. [Stress in every shape and form is bad for people] [because it can kill]. [The first scientist [who uncovered the relationship between stress and health] was Hans Selye]. [This was back in early 20th century]. [Selye found] [that stress is linked to the perception of danger in our lives]. For example, [when animals are being hunted] [they get a rush of stress] [which allows them to run away to safety] [**or** they can fight for their life]. [At first, doctors doubted] [that stress had any effect on the physical body], [**but** in the 1950s, medical scientists discovered] [that stress can cause coronary disease]. [Basing their studies on people with different personalities]. [They discovered] [that the body was in the constant state of fight-or-flight], [if the person was always angry]. [This condition resulted in health problems]. [Stress is inevitable] [**but** there are ways to control it], [**and** the first thing [one must do] is not to be angry].	There are four FANBOYS: Or But And But All come between independent clauses → insert commas where they are missing; keep commas where they are present.

Corrections based on Step 3
For example, [when animals are being hunted] [they get a rush of stress] [which allows them to run away to safety], [**or** they can fight for their life].
[Stress is inevitable], [**but** there are ways to control it], [**and** the first thing [one must do] is not to be angry].

Step 4: Circle or highlight all the subordinating words at the beginning of the bracketed clauses (*when, because, if, after, before, that,* etc.)
[The article states] [**that** everyone on the planet experiences stress]. [Stress in every shape and form is bad for people] [**because** it can kill]. [The first scientist [who uncovered the relationship between stress and health] was Hans Selye]. [This was back in early 20th century]. [Selye found] [**that** stress is linked to the perception of danger in our lives]. For example, [**when** animals are being hunted] [they get a rush of stress] [which allows them to run away to safety] [or they can fight for their life].
[At first, doctors doubted] [**that** stress had any effect on the physical body], [but in the 1950s, medical scientists discovered] [**that** stress can cause coronary disease]. [Basing their studies on people with different personalities]. [They discovered] [**that** the body was in the constant state of fight-or-flight], [**if** the person was always angry]. [This condition resulted in health problems]. [Stress is inevitable] [but there are ways to control it], [and the first thing [one must do] is not to be angry].

Step 5: Check if the clause with the subordinator in it comes before or after the main clause. If it is before the main clause, put a comma after it. If it is after the main clause, make sure there is <u>no</u> comma before it.

Text	Editing Notes
[The article states] [**that** everyone on the planet experiences stress].	That-clause after main clause → no comma
[Stress in every shape and form is bad for people] [**because** it can kill].	Because-clause after main clause → no comma
[Selye found] [**that** stress is linked to the perception of danger in our lives].	That-clause after the main clause → no comma
...[**when** animals are being hunted], [they get a rush of stress]	When-clause before the main clause → insert a comma after the when-clause
[At first, doctors doubted] [**that** stress had any effect on the physical body]...	That-clause after the main clause → no comma
...medical scientists discovered] [**that** stress can cause coronary disease].	That-clause after the main clause → no comma
[They discovered] [**that** the body was in the constant state of fight-or-flight], [**if** the person was always angry].	That-clause after the main clause → no comma
...the body was in the constant state of fight-or-flight]¬[**if** the person was always angry].	If-clause after the main clause → delete the comma

Step 6: Highlight or circle all instances of "who" or "which" at the beginning of clauses.

[The article states] [that everyone on the planet experiences stress]. [Stress in every shape and form is bad for people] [because it can kill]. [The first scientist [**who** uncovered the relationship between stress and health] was Hans Selye]. [This was back in early 20th century]. [Selye found] [that stress is linked to the perception of danger in our lives]. For example, [when animals are being hunted] [they get a rush of stress] [**which** allows them to run away to safety] [or they can fight for their life].

[At first, doctors doubted] [that stress had any effect on the physical body], [but in the 1950s, medical scientists discovered] [that stress can cause coronary disease]. [Basing their studies on people with different personalities]. [They discovered] [that the body was in the constant state of fight-or-flight], [if the person was always angry]. [This condition resulted in health problems]. [Stress is inevitable] [but there are ways to control it], [and the first thing [one must do] is not to be angry].

Steps 7 and 8: Decide if the who- and which-clauses describe something unique (must have a comma) or add essential information to distinguish the thing they describe from other such things.	
Text	**Editing Notes**
[The first scientist [**who** uncovered the relationship between stress and health] was Hans Selye].	The who-clause distinguishes Hans Selye from other scientists. He is the one who uncovered the relationship between stress and health → no comma; keep as is
...[they get a rush of stress] ,[**which** allows them to run away to safety] [or they can fight for their life].	The which-clause describes a unique phenomenon of getting a rush of stress; it comments on the whole preceding idea → insert a comma
Step 9: If you find a segment that does not express a complete idea, but it is punctuated like a complete sentence, join it to another sentence.	
[Basing their studies on people with different personalities]. [They discovered] [that the body was in the constant state of fight-or-flight], [if the person was always angry]. → Basing their studies on people with different personalities, they discovered that the body was in the constant state of fight-or-flight, if the person was always angry.	First clause is not a complete sentence → attach it to the next sentence

Appendix D: Frequently Confused Words

Some words in English sound similar or identical but are spelled differently, are different parts of speech, and/or have different meanings. Other words have similar meanings but don't sound similar. As you develop a more specific vocabulary as a writer, review this list to make sure you are using the meaning a nd spelling that communicates your ideas clearly to your readers.

accept, except
- *Accept* is a verb that means *to receive willingly* or *to believe*.
    - Example: LeBron James <u>accepted</u> a more lucrative offer from a competing team.
    - Example: Teenagers must <u>accept</u> that nothing is ever completely deleted once it is sent or posted online.
- *Except* means *not including*.
    - Example: New Orleans abolished bail for all misdemeanor suspects, <u>except</u> people arrested for domestic violence, battery, impersonating a police officer, and carrying an illegal weapon.
    - Example: Many people on the internet claim to be tolerant, <u>except</u> when they encounter someone who disagrees with them.

adapt, adopt
- *Adapt* means modify or adjust.
    - Example: Due to the pandemic, Americans had to <u>adapt</u> to new working conditions.
- *Adopt* means 1) to choose to start, use, or follow or 2) to legally take and raise as one's own.
    - Example: With changing work expectations, more companies are <u>adopting</u> optional work-from-home policies.
    - Example: Humane societies hope that people will <u>adopt</u> pets rather than buying them from pet stores.

advice, advise
- *Advice* is a noun that means guidance.
  - Example: Young professionals seek financial _advice_ to help them pay off student loans, save for future goals, and plan retirement.
- *Advise* is a verb that means to guide.
  - Example: The President's Cabinet should _advise_ the President on their area of specialty.

affect, effect
- *Affect* is a verb that means to make a difference or to touch emotionally.
  - Example: Tropical storms, especially monsoons and cyclones, regularly _affect_ coastal regions.
- *Effect* is a noun that means a change or result.
  - Example: Hunger and lack of sleep have a negative _effect_ on students' ability to process new information.

allude, elude
- *Allude* means to suggest or to mention briefly.
  - Example: Adolescents _allude_ to personal aspects to justify their alcohol intake.
  - Example: The author _alludes_ to the Biblical story of Adam and Eve when he mentions "forbidden fruit."]
- *Elude* means 1) to escape from or 2) to fail to achieve or attain something.
  - Example: The gunman _eluded_ police officers initially, but they later arrested him at his home.
  - Example: Although they tried a regular sleep routine, meditation, and light regulation, sleep _eluded_ them.

a lot
- *A lot* is always two words, not one. However, you should usually use a more specific word in academic and professional writing.

amount, number
- Both words describe how much or how many. Generally, *amount* is used for things that cannot be counted, and *number* is used for things that can be counted.
  - Example: Vacation options are limited by the _amount_ of money people have available.
  - Example: An unexpected _number_ of people joined the rally.

assistants, assistance
- *Assistants* means helpers.

- Example: The researcher recruited two graduate students as *assistants*.
- *Assistance* means help.
  - Example: The two graduate students gave *assistance* on the research study.

brake, break

- *Brake* means to slow to a stop.
  - Example: Leaving a space between cars is important in case drivers *brake* abruptly.
- *Break* generally means 1) to separate into pieces, 2) to interrupt, or 3) to pause an activity.
  - Example: Stores adopted policies of "you *break* it; you buy it."
  - Example: Kelly Clarkson grew up in a small town and wanted to *break* away.

capital, capitol

- *Capital* means 1) the city of a region with its government and administrative center or 2) larger letters.
  - Example: The *capital* of India used to be called Bombay.
- *Capitol* means government buildings.
  - Example: Congress meets at *Capitol* Hill.

cite, sight, site

- *Cite* is a verb that means to give credit.
  - Example: The English professor reminded students again to *cite* their sources in their research project.
- *Sight* means vision.
  - Example: The patient lost her sense of *sight* after the accident.
- *Site* means location.
  - Example: The student filming crew were scouting a *site* for their project.

clothes, close, cloths

- *Clothes* means items covering the body.
  - Example: Loose-fitting *clothes* should not be worn around the machinery.
- *Close* means the opposite of open or to end.
  - Example: Trading was put on hold at the *close* of the market Thursday.
- *Cloths* means fabrics.
  - Example: The clothes designer prefers fine linen *cloths*.

complement, compliment
- *Complement* means to add to something to improve, enhance, or perfect something.
  - Example: With copyright restrictions, some YouTubers and podcasters write their own music to <u>complement</u> their content.
- *Compliment* means to politely congratulate or praise.
  - Example: Workers in sales may <u>compliment</u> customers on their clothing or intelligence to form an emotional connection.

could of, may of, must of, should of, would of
- *Of* sounds the same as the shortened version of have: *'ve*. However, the word *of* never follows could, may, must, should, or would. Instead, write *have* in academic or professional settings or *'ve* in informal settings.
  - Example: Exceptional students assess what they <u>should have</u> done differently in their classes so they can improve in the future.

council, counsel
- *Council* is a noun that means a group of people who advise or make decisions.
  - Example: The student <u>council</u> suggested that the homecoming dance should be held outdoors.
- *Counsel* means advise (verb) or advice (noun).
  - Example: The advisor <u>counseled</u> the incoming freshmen to plan to graduate on time.

desert, dessert
- *Desert* means 1) a dry area of land or 2) to abandon.
  - Example: The Sahara is the world's largest <u>desert</u>.
  - Example: The soldier <u>deserted</u> his unit and fled to the rear.
- *Dessert* means a sweet dish.
  - Example: Mochi is a traditional Japanese <u>dessert</u>.

elicit, illicit
- *Elicit* is a verb that means to evoke or get a response.
  - Example: Student teachers practice writing essay questions that <u>elicit</u> useful answers from future students.
- *Illicit* means forbidden.
  - Example: The officer discovered <u>illicit</u> drugs in the suspect's car.

ensure, insure
- *Ensure* means to make certain.
  - Example: During the first week of school, students should arrive at campus early to <u>ensure</u> they can find parking.

- *Insure* means to secure or protect against.
    - Example: When buying a car with a loan, consumers are required to *insure* their vehicle to cover the cost in case of damage.

everyday, every day
- *Everyday* means ordinary or used daily.
    - Example: Charging smartphones is an *everyday* occurrence for nearly every young adult.
- *Every day* means daily.
    - Example: Americans use their smartphones *every* single *day* in our society.

fewer, less
- *Fewer* is used for items that can be counted.
    - Example: A large number of people would benefit from consuming *fewer* calories.
- *Less* is used for items that can't be counted.
    - Example: For decades, food packaging counseled consumers to eat *less* fat.

imply, infer
- *Imply* means to suggest.
    - Example: The writer's word choice *implies* that she is angry with the situation she describes.
- *Infer* means to conclude.
    - Example: We can *infer* from the data that the law is not resulting in the desired outcome.

its, it's
- *Its* means belonging to it.
    - Example: The moon has *its* own resources.
- It's means it is or it has.
    - Example: *It's* important to check the sources of information online.

lay, lie
- *Lay* means to put something else down.
    - Example: The neonatal nurses were taught to carefully *lay* the infants down.
- *Lie* means to recline or put oneself down. (*Lay* is also a verb form of *lie*).
    - Example: If the client feels dizzy after the exercise, he should *lie* down.

lead, led
- *Lead* is a verb that means to guide. (It rhymes with *need*). *Lead* is also a noun that means a type of metal. (It rhymes with *head*).
  - Example: The team captain will <u>lead</u> the women's soccer team to victory.
  - Example: Homebuyers prefer copper pipes instead of <u>lead</u> pipes.
- *Led* is a verb form of *lead*. (It rhymes with *head*).
  - Example: The team captain <u>led</u> the women's soccer team to victory last year.

lose, loose
- *Lose* is a verb that means 1) to misplace or 2) not win.
  - Example: If employees <u>lose</u> their ID card, they have to pay a fee to replace it.
- *Loose* means not tight or not secure.
  - Example: Safety regulations do not allow <u>loose</u> clothing around the machinery.

maybe, may be
- *Maybe* means perhaps.
  - Example: <u>Maybe</u> it failed because they changed targets at the last minute.
- *May be* means might be.
  - Example: The cost of the project <u>may be</u> higher than we expected.

many, much
- *Many* is for items that can be counted.
  - Example: <u>Many</u> programmers teach themselves.
- *Much* is for items that can't be counted.
  - Example: Most young people want to make as <u>much</u> money as they can.

passed, past
- *Passed* is a verb form of *pass* that means 1) to go by something or 2) to hand an object to someone.
  - Example: The vehicles in the carpool lane <u>passed</u> all the stopped traffic.
  - Example: The presenter <u>passed</u> handouts to the audience members.
- *Past* is a noun that means a time before today. Past also means 1) a direction or 2) beyond something else.
  - Example: The vehicles in the carpool lane drove <u>past</u> all the stopped traffic. (Notice the verb "drove" in the sentence.)

- Example: When students look *past* the stress of classes to their ultimate goals, they can overcome most of the challenges they face. (Notice the verb "look" in the sentence.)

patients, patience
- *Patients* means people receiving medical treatment.
  - Example: New *patients* have to fill out forms with their medical history.
- *Patience* means tolerating without getting upset.
  - Example: Voters are losing *patience* with slow-moving policy changes.

peace, piece
- *Peace* means tranquility or no war.
  - Example: The *peace* treaty had positive effects on the economy and safety.
- *Piece* means part of a whole or a unit.
  - Example: The genome is like a gigantic *piece* of software that runs numerous sections in parallel.

percent, percentage
- *Percent* is used after a number, and *percentage* is not.
  - Example: Civil servants will have an average pay increase of 2.7 *percent*.
  - Example: This *percentage* is comparable to increases for elected officials.

precede, proceed
- *Precede* means to come before.
  - Example: The anomalies *precede* the American Revolutionary War.
- *Proceed* means to begin or continue on.
  - Example: The patient decided to *proceed* with chemotherapy.

principal, principle
- *Principal* means 1) primary or foremost or 2) the person with the highest authority.
  - Example: Despite the original intention, quitting cigarettes is not the *principal* use of vaping.
- *Principle* means a fundamental truth or guiding rule.
  - Example: Water conservation is the central *principle* behind the product.

quite, quiet
- *Quite* means somewhat or completely.
  - Example: Horse prices were *quite* low compared to previous years.
- *Quiet* means with little noise or discretely.

- Example: The Department of Motor Vehicles provides a *quiet* environment for taking a driver's license test.

respectfully, respectively
- *Respectfully* means with politeness or admiration.
    - Example: Productive communication allows opposing sides to *respectfully* disagree with each other.
- *Respectively* means individually in the order they were mentioned.
    - Example: The defendant and his collaborator received sentences of one year and eight months, *respectively*.

since, sense
- *Since* means 1) from a time in the past or 2) because.
    - Example: It has been 40 years *since* a human traveled beyond a low Earth orbit.
    - Example: *Since* the majority of the scientific community agrees on this issue, the theory is credible.
- *Sense* means 1) a feeling or 2) sight, smell, hearing, taste, and touch.
    - Example: Graphic designers have the *sense* that their clients do not understand the limits of Photoshop.
    - Example: Lacking a *sense* of smell can be dangerous in some job settings.

than, then
- *Than* is used for comparing.
    - Example: The gains are clearly greater *than* the losses.
- *Then* means after that or at that time.
    - Example: They get what they want, and *then* they're gone.

their, they're, there
- *Their* means something belongs to them.
    - Example: Tests should prompt students to reveal *their* understanding of the class material.
- *They're* means they are.
    - Example: *They're* concerned that we're on the edge of a thermonuclear war.
    - Example: *They're* trying to address their concerns through diplomacy.
- *There* usually means in, at, or to that place or position.
    - Example: In the future the technology will evolve, but they're not *there* yet.
    - Example: *There* is credible evidence to support their theory.

too, two, to
- *Too* means 1) also or 2) excessively.

- Example: Students may be surprised to know that teachers can have test anxiety, _too_.
- Example: When small children talk _too_ fast, they can be difficult to understand.
- *Two* means the number.
  - Example: One online news portal has the readership of over _two_ million visitors per month.
- *To* usually means 1) a direction or 2) part of a verb form.
  - Example: Many children like _to_ go _to_ the park _to_ play outside.

weather, whether
- *Weather* means the state of the atmosphere or temperature outside.
  - Example: Sunny _weather_ draws senior citizens, known as snowbirds, to locations in the southern United States during winter months.
- *Whether* means if.
  - Example: There is a heated debate about _whether_ social media use has more positive or more negative effects on young adults' mental health.

who's, whose
- *Who's* means who is.
  - Example: _Who's_ planning to attend office hours?
- *Whose* means belonging to which person.
  - Example: _Whose_ idea was it to make attendance mandatory?

woman, women
- *Woman* means one adult female. *Women* means more than one.
  - Example: Beyoncé shared in an interview that she loves being a _woman_ and being a friend to other women.
  - Example: Millions of _women_ and girls around the world experience poverty and social exclusion.

your, you're
- *Your* means that something belongs to you.
  - Example: Don't forget to turn in _your_ assignment.
- *You're* means you are.
  - Example: _You're_ working hard, so you should take a break.
- In academic and professional settings, writers should typically only use *you* and *your* (also called second person) when writing to a specific person or group. Instead of using *you* to mean everyone, be more specific.

Index

CPSIA information can be obtained
at www.ICGtesting.com
Printed in the USA
LVHW060023260523
748075LV00008B/71

9 780367 748593